BIRDS

ROB HUME

HAMLYN

HOW TO USE THIS BOOK

This guide covers over 200 species of bird likely to be seen in the UK, plus some rare visitors. In the identification pages (40-125) they are listed broadly by family, though some unrelated species may be grouped together. The text gives the English name, the length (L) in centimetres, and some useful information, on plumage or habits, for example. In general, the illustrations show the adult male; where others are shown, ♀ means female, ♂ means male, and juv a juvenile or immature bird. S, W, A and Sp mean summer, winter, autumn and spring respectively. On the distribution maps, purple indicates where species live all-year round, red the summer breeding areas, blue the winter areas, and yellow the migration areas.

HOODED CROW
L 47cm. Same species as carrion crow; grey and black. Lazy flight.

ACKNOWLEDGEMENTS

The author and publishers would like to thank the following individuals for their assistance in the preparation of this book: Andrew Branson of British Wildlife Publishing, Principal Consultant · David Christie, Editorial Consultant · and Derek Hall, who conceived the series.

Published in 1991 by
Hamlyn Children's Books,
part of Reed International Books,
Michelin House, 81 Fulham Road,
London SW3 6RB

ISBN 0 600 56948 9

Printed in Portugal

CONTENTS

BIRD CHARACTERISTICS

There is such a variety of habitat and food available to birds that they have adapted to a great many lifestyles. Evolution over millions of years has developed birds that are ideal for wet places, some that live in woods, some that live in open spaces, and others that spend their lives over the sea. To do this, though, they all have to be specially fitted to take advantage of the food and nest sites that the habitat offers, and to withstand the weather and other hardships that they face. They also have plumage patterns to help them hide, or help them attract mates, or find each other when feeding or roosting.

Peregrines dive headlong to kill other birds, striking with their strong feet and curved, sharp claws.

Swifts live nearly all their lives in the air, gliding on long, slender wings which give little wind resistance.

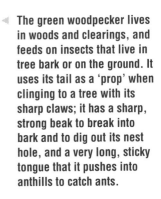

The green woodpecker lives in woods and clearings, and feeds on insects that live in tree bark or on the ground. It uses its tail as a 'prop' when clinging to a tree with its sharp claws; it has a sharp, strong beak to break into bark and to dig out its nest hole, and a very long, sticky tongue that it pushes into anthills to catch ants.

Make a feather collection. Experts can often tell a bird just from one or two feathers. Collect any feathers that you find in the countryside. Look for them especially in the autumn, when birds are moulting, and at the edges of woods and parks where birds are killed by cats or hawks. Beaches and edges of lakes are good spots, as feathers collect on the strandline. Clean them and keep them mounted on pieces of card, with details of the place and date. Identify as many as you can using books and photographs. If you can't tell what they are, wait until you find out rather than guess.

Greenfinches have thick, ▷ strong bills to split husks from seeds; the green colours give them good camouflage.

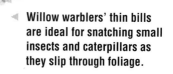

Willow warblers' thin bills are ideal for snatching small insects and caterpillars as they slip through foliage.

Waterproof feathers, with ▽ dense down beneath, and broad, webbed feet, make the mallard ideal for swimming.

Wet mud is full of worms; ▲ the snipe's bill probes into it to catch them, and its long toes stop it from sinking in.

EQUIPMENT

BINOCULARS

Try binoculars before you buy them. Find a pair that you can hold comfortably – not too big. The numbers on binoculars show the magnification and the width of the lenses in millimetres: 8×30, 8×40, 10×40 or 10×50 are ideal (but the last are big and heavy). The bigger the lens, the brighter the view. Look at a post or sign. Cover the right lens and focus the left using the central wheel. Then keep that still, and, looking through the right eye, focus the right lens on the same object with the eyepiece adjustment. This will 'balance' any difference between your eyes. The eyepiece setting should be kept the same: now you need use only the centre wheel to adjust for different distances.

Check for alignment – make sure you don't 'see double'. And make sure that the binoculars don't bend the picture around the edges too much, and that there are no bright edges of red or blue around TV aerials or poles against the sky. Get the best for what you can afford to pay; they will last for years.

Binoculars are your most expensive and most useful piece of equipment – look after them. Always use the neck strap. Most of all, learn to use them properly, otherwise you will have spent money for nothing. When you spot a bird, keep looking at it and raise the binoculars to your eyes – don't look down at them and swing them from side to side until you see what you are after! Use the focusing wheel properly instead of straining your eyes. Relax your eyes and turn the wheel until the image is sharp.

◄ Telescopes with tripods are big, heavy and very expensive, but they are great for seeing birds at very long range. A tripod helps you get a steady view and lets other people take a turn, too. Go for telescopes magnifying 20 to 40 times, with a lens at least 60mm wide – so, 20×60, 40×60 or 30×75 would be ideal. In a wood or park, a telescope is no use – leave it behind.

Wear the right kind of ▷ clothes – comfortable and warm, and waterproof. It is hopeless going out if you get cold and wet – you won't see much and won't enjoy it! Colour is less important, but try for green or something dark. Find a coat with plenty of pockets that doesn't rustle. Take a bag, pencil and notebook, maps, and lunchbox.

FIELDCRAFT

Birdwatching isn't difficult, but can seem like it. Part of the problem is seeing the birds before they see you and fly away! It is partly common sense. Get out and enjoy yourself with other people – no-one would suggest that birdwatching needs total silence and no fun – but if you really want to see birds, it is best to be quiet. Walk slowly, wear suitably-coloured clothes and *keep looking around*. Don't just look at your friends and talk – look for movements, shadows, reflections; listen for bird calls and songs; and try to anticipate where birds will be.

The sun behind you gives good light; but look through a hedge or trees against the light in winter to spot birds against the bright sky. Then carefully move around to get a better view. Remember, even pale birds look almost black against a bright sky.

Keep below the skyline if you can; don't walk on raised banks. Try to keep bushes or banks behind you to prevent a sharp outline; approach good spots, such as muddy pools or a good beach, behind bushes, hedges, fences or buildings, then peer round carefully.

DIRECTIONS

Try to find good landmarks, such as a prominent tree, so you can point birds out to friends. If there are none, use the 'clock face': a bird dead ahead is '12 o'clock', to the left '9 o'clock', to the right '3 o'clock' and so on. Or a bird down to the left of a treetop can be '7' or '8 o'clock'. Talk quietly. Even quiet, deep voices carry, but high shouts are the worst. Whisper gently – loud hisses are just as bad as shouting!

If a bird goes into the ▲ middle of a thick bush, don't charge in after it. Go slowly; sit quietly and wait for it to come out again, or go quietly to the other side in case it goes right through. A bird in a reedbed needs patience – never crash in to look for it.

Edges of woods and ▲ edges of clearings and fields are good for birds; so, too, are sides of lakes, ditches and streams. When you approach any such line, go slowly, and look both ways before the birds fly off.

Be an Indian scout looking for birds: don't walk on noisy gravel or dead leaves, or tread on brittle twigs. Birds see you move sideways most easily, so approach in a straight line, slowly, evenly. Move away just as carefully when you have finished, too.

ATTRACTING BIRDS

Instead of trying to stalk birds to get close, why not get them to come closer to you? It is great fun to try it, and often gives good results. Three things help: food, water and a place to nest. A fourth is patience. You may need to give them time to get used to your new ideas. In a garden, a bird bath, or better still a pond, will make a world of difference. Birds need to bathe and drink often, even in the bitterest winter. Make a pond with shallow edges and stones so that birds can walk in or lean over to drink. Keep it clean and fresh – a garden centre will advise you on special plants that will help – and try not to let it freeze in winter.

Water is great for ▼ starlings, sparrows, thrushes and finches all year. Look for warblers, especially young ones in the early autumn. They come to bathe a lot. Keep an eye open early in the morning, when you may see something special at your pond, such as a jay, or even a sparrowhawk taking a bath! Keep a notebook of 'pond birds'.

Some birds, such as the ▼ goldcrest (below) and the treecreeper, will not come to birdtables. You can help them, and attract them closer, by smearing cheese and fat, or wedging currants and berries, into rough bark; even honey is good!

Nuthatches do visit ▼ peanut bags, but like nuts and berries wedged into bark or put into holes drilled in an old log. Experiment.

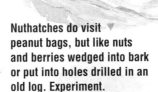

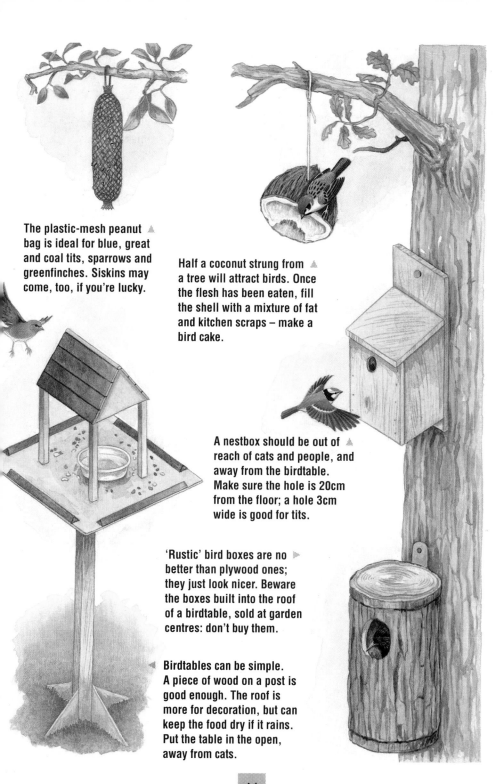

The plastic-mesh peanut bag is ideal for blue, great and coal tits, sparrows and greenfinches. Siskins may come, too, if you're lucky.

Half a coconut strung from a tree will attract birds. Once the flesh has been eaten, fill the shell with a mixture of fat and kitchen scraps – make a bird cake.

A nestbox should be out of reach of cats and people, and away from the birdtable. Make sure the hole is 20cm from the floor; a hole 3cm wide is good for tits.

'Rustic' bird boxes are no better than plywood ones; they just look nicer. Beware the boxes built into the roof of a birdtable, sold at garden centres: don't buy them.

Birdtables can be simple. A piece of wood on a post is good enough. The roof is more for decoration, but can keep the food dry if it rains. Put the table in the open, away from cats.

PLANNING A TRIP

CAREFUL PREPARATION

There are many helpful items for getting the best out of your birdwatching trip. Look at the TV weather forecast – frost may attract birds to the reservoir; strong winds will blow seabirds inshore; fog brings down migrants on the coast. Use Ordnance Survey 1:50,000 maps to find footpaths and woods, for example – even phone boxes and car parks are shown. If you go to the coast, check the times of tides first: use the local newspaper, or telephone the coastguard or harbour. Find a local bird-club report and see which places are good for birds, and when: a library will help. Try to get out early; birds go quiet later on.

Estuaries
If you go to an estuary, be there an hour or two before high tide. If there is a choice – with roads on both sides of a lake, for example – go where you can look west in the morning and east in the afternoon, so as not to look into the sun. If you want a long walk, try to get to a bus stop and ride back: that way you can cover twice the distance on foot. And go birdwatching with a friend – it's safer and more fun!

At a high-tide roost, get ▷ there before the birds, and sit down out of sight. Try a sloping grassy bank: it keeps you below the skyline. Don't stand up and walk away before the tide goes out again: you will scare all the birds, and they need to rest. Best of all, go to a nature reserve and look from a special hide. The RSPB publishes a list of its reserves you can visit, as will your local county trust.

◁ Many birds come out at night, so plan a trip at dusk. Go to a wood in May or June and look for woodcocks over the trees – you will hear them first. Nightjars (left) are rare birds of lowland heaths; they start to 'churr' in summer just after sunset. Remember your way back in the dark! It is best to go with a bird-club group or with your parents.

CODE OF CONDUCT

The well-being of the bird always comes first. Try not to disturb it. Try never to scare up roosting flocks. If a bird disappears into a thicket or reedbed, it is best to forget it rather than chase in after it and damage the habitat. If you see a baby bird (such as this juvenile robin), never pick it up; leave it for its parent, which will be waiting nearby. It will not be lost, but simply calling to be fed. Never trespass, trample crops or leave gates open.

MAKING FIELD NOTES

Sketching birds makes you look carefully at them, and makes you work quickly. Make an outline sketch and add in special features that catch your eye – like stripes over the eye, bars of colour on the wing, or streaks on the breast. Then write labels on all the parts of the bird with arrows to the parts you mean. This will make you look at all of it, and you must not miss any out. That way, you should note down all you need to tell what bird it is later. Make your notes simple, but as accurate as you can. For a common tern in summer, you might do a sketch like the one shown below.

Notes
These are the sort of notes you should write on your sketchpad:

Slim, graceful bird
Sharp, thin beak
Tiny red legs

Make a note, too, of the location of your sighting, the time of day, the date, and any other significant information, such as the day's weather conditions.

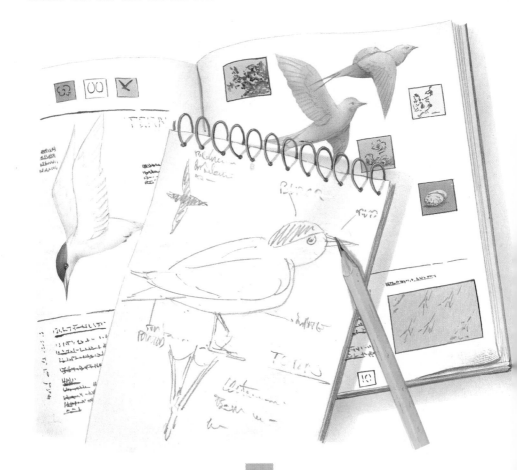

Actions ▷

Look for flight pattern – straight or wavering, flat or swooping? Watch for wing- and tail-flicking, or up-and-down tail bobbing; and any special feeding actions, such as tugging berries on bush, probing into grass, or poking beak into water.

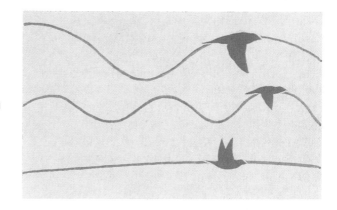

Shapes ▷

Look for special shapes of bills, wings, tail – and compare with other birds you already know. Is its bill triangular like a sparrow's, thin like a robin's, long like a heron's or flat like a duck's?

Special signs ▽

Some birds leave distinctive droppings, or remains of their feeding. In autumn, look for loose feathers where birds have been moulting, such as those from gulls on playing fields or lakes.

◁ Pellets and droppings

Some birds leave pellets (coughed up through the mouth) where they roost, or after they have fed, such as owls. It is sometimes possible to see what food the bird has been eating.

Footprints ▷

You may find footprints on mud near the water's edge, or in snow. They're hard to identify! In mud by the sea, you might see where waders have been probing with their bills. Although you may not be able to identify the species, you will know where the birds are active, and can plan another visit there.

PHOTOGRAPHY

Taking photographs of wild birds is a real challenge, so don't expect fantastic results right away. Above all you need patience, and you need to be able to keep still and quiet. Even with long lenses, you have to get close to birds, and that means stalking them very carefully indeed, or making a hide and keeping out of sight. Birdwatching hides at nature reserves are okay, but often don't get you really close enough to the birds. Try colour prints first; use 'fast' film (a local camera shop will help you), such as 100 or 200 or even 400 ISO. You usually need a fast shutter speed – such as 1/250th of a second – to freeze movement. A tripod helps keep the camera steady.

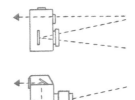

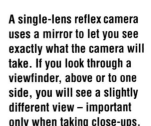

A single-lens reflex camera uses a mirror to let you see exactly what the camera will take. If you look through a viewfinder, above or to one side, you will see a slightly different view – important only when taking close-ups.

A long cable-release helps to stop shaking or jogging of the camera as you press the shutter. With a long lead you can take pictures from several metres away, but then you will need a motordrive – which can be noisy – to wind the film on.

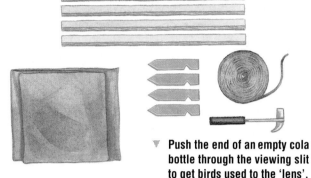

▼ Push the end of an empty cola bottle through the viewing slit to get birds used to the 'lens'.

A hide will let you sit beside your garden pond, or by a woodland clearing, and birds will not know you are there! Just put up a framework of four solid posts. Tie them down with guy ropes if needed. Then find some dull, greenish hessian or canvas – something that won't rustle – and make a square 'tent' with an entrance flap, a viewing slit, and some pegs to fasten it tight. Make sure it doesn't flap in the wind.

PROJECT

Borrow a camera if you can, if you don't own one. Get some colour-print film and have a go at photography. Garden birds make good subjects, but birds on the park lake or at the coast may be more interesting – this rook is a typical farmland bird. Gulls on the pier or following ships give you plenty of chances to take pictures, but they are not so easy as they look! Don't get too carried away or you will use all your film in one go. The main thing, at first, is to get the bird focused, well exposed (not too dark or too light), and nice and big – which means getting close.

MIGRATION

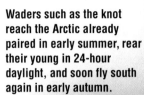

Waders such as the knot reach the Arctic already paired in early summer, rear their young in 24-hour daylight, and soon fly south again in early autumn.

Some starlings move long distances from eastern Europe, where the winters are harsh, to the milder west; others spend their lives in one small area unless a big freeze-up forces them south.

A WONDER OF NATURE

Birds can move long distances in a short time, and can cross the sea. They take advantage of food supplies that may be present only in one season, or avoid the harsh northern winter by flying south in autumn. The northern summer is rich in insect life, with long days that allow birds to feed almost around-the-clock. Such conditions are too good for insect-eating birds to miss, but, when cold, dark winters arrive, they move out to find easier conditions elsewhere – so migration evolved. It is one of nature's greatest wonders.

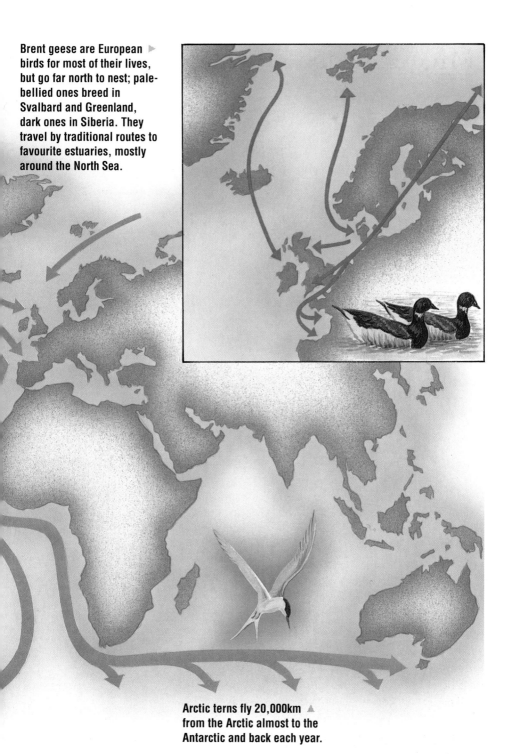

Brent geese are European
birds for most of their lives,
but go far north to nest; pale-
bellied ones breed in
Svalbard and Greenland,
dark ones in Siberia. They
travel by traditional routes to
favourite estuaries, mostly
around the North Sea.

Arctic terns fly 20,000km
from the Arctic almost to the
Antarctic and back each year.

GARDENS AND PARKS

There is nowhere better to get to know birds than in your garden or, if you don't have one, in the nearest park. They will often be tame – even 'shy' ones like woodpigeons and gulls get used to people – and you can watch them closely. Feeding them helps bring the birds close. Parks are great places for taking photographs, too. The birds are not all just sparrows and pigeons, either: a good town park with a lake can easily have 20 or 30 species, and over a year you will see many more.

Blackbird ▼
Males are jet-black with a yellow bill, but females are brown – though still much darker than other thrushes.

Robin
Adults, of both sexes, are the same all year, but look for spotted young ones in summer. ▶

Black-headed gull ▲
Summer adults with dark brown heads are not so common as winter birds, with black 'ear spots' on whiter heads.

◀ Moorhen
Watch the way its head bobs forward and back as it swims, with tail up and shoulders low.

Mallards hatch their chicks early in the ▶ year. They lead them to water – any pond or ditch will do – but many are killed by dogs, pike and other predators. Watch mallard families and record how many young survive.

Collared dove ▶
A common, tame, pale dove, sandy-grey or dull brownish with a black collar over the back of the neck.

Greenfinch ▲
Only summer males are bright apple-green; they otherwise can look dull, olive or brownish, with some yellow in the wings and tail.

Blue tit ▲
A classic peanut-bag bird, tiny and quick, bluest in spring. Note its blue cap outlined with a ring of white.

Dunnock ▶
Small, quiet, shuffling and easy to miss, dunnocks have a high, thin, squeaky call.

◀ Pied wagtail
The pied wagtail feeds on lawns, tarmac paths and roads. Its long tail often flicks up and down.

TOWNS

There are more birds in towns and big cities than you might expect. Even in Central London, a kestrel may fly overhead, twisting between the skyscrapers. In many Continental towns there will be the songs of black redstarts before the noise of morning traffic. In the United States, peregrines have nested on tall buildings, and in Europe they may one day do the same. In winter, puddles on footpaths are visited by starlings, jackdaws and especially pied wagtails, and you may be lucky enough to see a grey wagtail. House martins are becoming more common again.

Kestrel ▲
Kestrels nest on high office blocks and cathedrals; they catch sparrows in the streets and parks, or steal scraps.

◄ Magpie
In many suburban gardens magpies have become quite common, adding colour and life to the scene.

▼ Pied wagtail
Only in winter can you hope for a glimpse of a pied wagtail, pausing at a pond or flying up from a puddle.

House sparrow ▲
Of all the town birds, the house sparrow is the best known, cheeky and noisy, full of life and energy.

Starling roosts in towns ▶ are spectacular, but how do you count them? On ledges or wires they are not so bad – count them in fives or tens. In flight, practice is the key: split the flock into tens, then fifties if it is really big, and try to go quickly through it – 50, 100, 150, 200, 250, 300...

Pigeon ▶
Town pigeons are common, tame and very variable, patchy grey, black, white or brown. They nest on high ledges.

◀ **Black redstart**
Black redstarts are rare birds of towns and factory areas, feeding on rough land and nesting in buildings.

FARMLAND

Farmland has birds that also live in woods and open heaths; it is an artificial environment with birds of both. If the fields are very big, with no hedges and no ponds, there are few birds – just skylarks and maybe rooks (but even rooks have to go elsewhere to nest). Farm ponds used to be great for moorhens, ducks and wagtails, but most have been filled in. If there are still small fields, with hedges and scattered trees, you can find many more species: linnets, willow warblers, magpies, crows, blackbirds and mistle thrushes, and exciting birds such as little owls, kestrels and buzzards.

Stock dove ▼
Stock doves like farmland and old parks with plenty of big trees or ancient barns. They form flocks in winter.

▼ Yellowhammer
Long, hot summer days seem empty of birds, but the bright yellowhammer carries on singing all the time.

◄ Lapwing
Nowadays, few farms are wet enough for lapwings; they have become rare nesters, but are common in winter, in lowlands.

Magpie ▼
Magpies love overgrown, thick hedges where they can hide their big stick nests. They are real characters.

Kestrel ►
Although common in many places, kestrels are especially typical of farmland with hedges and tall trees.

Grey partridge ▼
Grey partridges prefer old meadows and cereal fields, but need strips of longer grass by hedgerows in which to feed.

WOODLAND

Woods are mostly very good for birds, but often frustrating for birdwatchers. In winter, bird flocks move around in search of food. If you can't find the flock, you see few birds. In summer most birds stop singing and become hard to see in the thick foliage. Spring is best, when birds are singing loudly and the leaves are not yet too thick and dark. Artificial conifer plantations have fewer birds than oak or beech woods, but native pine woods in northern Scotland and parts of Europe have really good species, from capercaillies and crossbills to ospreys and crested tits.

Great spotted woodpecker ▼
Woodpeckers feed on grubs under bark, chipping into it with their strong bills. They also chisel out nest holes.

▼ Treecreeper
No bird is more closely tied to its habitat than the treecreeper, always creeping about on tree bark.

Wren ▼
Wrens are tiny but have loud, fast, trilling songs. They nest in upturned tree roots and under overhanging banks.

Blackcap ▶
Blackcaps sing beautifully; they like woods with tall trees and plenty of leafy saplings growing up underneath.

Tawny owl ▶
Large holes in ivy-covered trees are ideal for nesting tawny owls. They may dive at people who climb to the nest.

Woodpigeon ▲
With more berries and acorns about in autumn, woodpigeons tend to nest late in the year when there is plenty of food.

PROJECT

Watch tit flocks – such as these blue tits and great tit – in the woods in winter. Each species has its favourite food and feeding technique, but they overlap. Great tits are often on big branches, the main trunk, or on the ground, eating big berries and seeds. Tiny coal tits feed on insects at the tips of the thinnest twigs.

FRESH WATER

Fresh water gives a birdwatcher many more chances to see birds than dry land does. Yellow wagtails like wet fields; reeds have sedge and reed warblers, reed buntings and moorhens. Mallards are common, even on small ditches, but other ducks are scarce except in winter, when teals like small patches of water with reeds and rushes. Tufted ducks like deeper pools; wigeons graze on shorter turf. This is the kind of place to look for a kingfisher, and a water rail may skulk through the reedmace at the water's edge.

Swallow ▶
Few birds are so elegant as the swallow. It dips to drink from the surface, and catches insects over rivers and lakes.

Grey heron ▲
Grey herons are patient hunters of fish, standing in the shallows ready to strike. But they nest in tall trees!

◀ Reed bunting
Male reed buntings repeat a short, monotonous song over and over again from a tall stem in a reedbed or marsh.

Canada goose ▶
Canada geese were
introduced from North
America but are now
common in the UK; they
are much rarer in most
other parts of Europe.

Coot ▼
Coots prefer more open
water than moorhens, where
they also dive more
frequently for food.

◀ Redshank
Redshanks nest in damp
grassland within easy reach
of muddy watersides. They
often perch on fenceposts
in the spring.

MARSHES

Marshland is a precious environment. As so much land is drained, marshes are becoming very scarce, and even such creatures as frogs are now rare. Marsh birds have suffered, too, and snipe have gone from most of lowland Britain. By the coast there may be breeding waders and marsh harriers, and in winter hen harriers and short-eared owls also hunt over marshes. Special marshes like dense reedbeds have real rarities such as bearded tits, bitterns and Savi's warblers; in the Netherlands they also have bluethroats, purple herons and spoonbills.

Black-headed gull ▼
Most gulls nest on cliffs and islands, but the black-headed gull likes lowland marshes as well as moorland pools.

Marsh harrier ▼
Marsh harriers nest in reeds and hunt for young birds and voles. They were very rare in the UK, but more pairs nest here now.

◀ **Lapwing**
The long, wispy crest identifies the lapwing. It is a bird of short, damp grass with good views all around.

Bearded tit ▼
The bearded tit nests and spends all winter in reeds, unless high numbers force some birds out to other places in winter.

Snipe ▼
The snipe breeds in marsh, wet grazing land and bogs. When flushed, it flies with a twisting flight.

Sedge warbler ▼
The excited, varied song of the sedge warbler helps separate it from the more sedate reed warbler.

PROJECT

Try to visit a coastal marsh, perhaps while on a summer holiday, and sit on a high bank and look out over the reeds. Listen for the high, 'pinging' calls of bearded tits and watch for them whirring over the reed tops like tiny pheasants. If families are being fed, they may ignore you and come very close, so long as you are still and quiet. Young ones have striped backs, whereas males have blue heads with black moustaches. What colour are their eyes?

ESTUARIES

Estuaries are thrilling places, with vast numbers of birds, but they are also big, flat, and difficult for a birdwatcher. The best bet is to find where the birds gather at high tide. Be there as the tide comes in – keep out of sight – and wait for the birds to come to you! You may need a telescope for some, but there will be many that come close enough. Enjoy seeing waders, ducks and geese that have come from Greenland, Iceland, Scandinavia and even far-off Siberia!

Curlew ▲
A large, streaky wader with a very long bill. Pale brown, but seems darker at a distance.

Common gull ▶
A medium-sized gull with grey back and wings, dull green legs and dark eyes.

Bar-tailed godwit ▶
This is a large wader of muddy shores. Paler than curlew, its bill is long, thin, faintly curved upwards.

Lesser black-backed gull ▲
This is a gull with very dark grey back and wings; head dark and streaky in winter; legs and bill yellow.

◀ Shelduck
A big, eyecatching duck with lots of bright white. Head dark, band of orange around chest. Look at the red bill.

Brent goose ▼
A small, very dark goose from Siberia. The head, neck and chest are black; vivid white rear end; Greenland birds are paler.

PROJECT

Try to visit an estuary and identify the gulls and waders you see there – this winter visitor is a grey plover. The gulls are simpler – but beware the young ones, which all look blotchy brown! Leave them until later. Waders are more easily identified in summer plumage, but luckily they get that in early spring. Why not go in April or May?

Waders ▼
Many wading birds feed in estuaries and on coastal mud-flats. At a distance they may be difficult to identify, but watching their ways of feeding may give you a clue.

ystercatcher ▶
easy-to-recognise
ack-and-white wader,
th bright orange bill. Very
isy. Groups call with
ud piping notes.

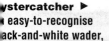

Turnstone ▲
Really does turn stones, looking for insects and shellfish beneath. Small, dumpy, very dark on top.

BIRDS AT SEA

Watching from a rocky headland in late summer is great for seabirds. In northern England, Wales or Scotland, you should see several different sorts. It is best to sit somewhere comfortable, safe (don't go close to the edge of cliffs), and out of the wind if you can: then watch and wait. Look out to sea with binoculars. Look to either side and spot birds coming towards you: it is hopeless spotting them out in front, because then they will already be going away! Birdwatching from a boat is great fun, especially in autumn. Watch the gulls in the slipstream!

Tern ▼
Terns are smaller than gulls, more slender, with long tails. Sandwich terns look skinny and very white; common terns are greyer; arctic terns are cleaner-looking, with the longest tails.

Gannet ▶
Adult gannets are big and brilliant white, but young ones look dark or blotchy. They glide a lot in the wind, but flap much more in calmer weather. They might plunge into the sea for fish.

Shag ▼
The shag is a big, dark bird with a 'snaky' head and neck. It dives beneath from the water surface, often with a little 'jump'.

◀ Guillemot
Guillemots swim underwater using their wings; you might see them from a cliff top if the water is clear.

Herring gull ▼
Gulls are broader-winged and squarer-tailed than terns; the herring gull is the typical seagull, pale grey and white, with loud squealing calls.

Skua ▲
Skuas are exciting and chase other birds for food. They look darker brown than young gulls, but arctic skuas can be white underneath.

Fulmar ▲
The fulmar is like a gull but, from above, only the head is white; the tail is grey. It has a stiff-flapping flight.

Cormorant ▲
Cormorants are bigger, thicker-billed and flatter-headed than shags.

Seabirds are seen best at ▶ their breeding colonies. Bird reserves are good places because they have safe viewpoints and paths. On cliffs it is vital to be safe and comfortable. Sit down and watch, and never creep down a slope, especially on grass, because it is very dangerous. Try to find a cove or inlet in the cliff, and look across at the birds on the other side.

MOORLAND

Birds of the moors tend to be shy and hard to see closely. Birds of prey such as hen harriers, merlins and peregrines are often away and out of sight almost before you get a good view. Even small birds, such as ring ouzels, keep out of sight beyond ridges or behind boulders, and grouse crouch down into long vegetation so you can walk right by them and never know it. But the moors are beautiful, full of interesting birds and worth the effort. Remember, though, that open moors can be dangerous, so be prepared for sudden bad weather.

Skylark ▲
Although common on lowland fields, skylarks are also birds of rough, upland moors where there is mixed grass and heather.

Stonechat ▼
Stonechats perch upright at the tops of stems and on wires. The black or brown chin is unlike a whinchat's.

Meadow pipit ▼
Meadow pipits creep quietly through grasses, but sing in the air, rising up and then dropping like a shuttlecock.

Stonechats and ▶
whinchats nest on moors.
Are whinchats (right)
commoner or rarer? What
habitats do they prefer? Look
for stonechats near gorse
and whinchats in bracken
and on bushy slopes – but
can you find either in young
conifer plantations?

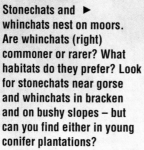

Hen harrier ▼
Heather moors with rushy
valleys are ideal for hen
harriers. They fly low,
hunting birds and voles.

Red grouse ▶
Red grouse are birds of
upland heather moors. They
are closely related to the
Continental willow grouse.

MOUNTAINS

These dramatic landscapes are not easy for birdwatching: a bird can be a mile across a valley before you know it, and you may not spot it again. But the effort is worthwhile if you see wheatears and ring ouzels, or birds such as merlins and peregrines. You may be incredibly lucky and see a golden eagle, probably just a dot over a distant peak. Look along mountain streams, too, for dippers and sandpipers.

Wheatear ▼
Wheatears like stony slopes with patches of short grass where they can feed.

◀ **Buzzard**
Buzzards are large, brown birds of prey, usually patterned with cream. They fly over woods and crags.

◄ Golden eagle
Golden eagles are the greatest mountain birds. They are very rarely seen closely – unlike buzzards – but usually soar high in the sky or float above a distant ridge. Look for the very long wings and longer tail and head than a buzzard's.

Peregrine ▼
To see a peregrine is a great treat; it looks 'anchor-shaped' overhead, with a short tail and swept-back wings, and may fold its wings back to dive in a 'stoop' after its prey.

Raven ▼
Ravens are huge crows, with very noisy, hard calls like 'crronk crronk'; you may see several together with luck. They are expert fliers.

Ring ouzel ▼
The ring ouzel is a mountain thrush, shy and elusive but best found by its loud, wild song in spring.

GREBES AND DIVERS

GREAT CRESTED GREBE
L 48cm. Tall, slim neck glistens white at front; in winter, head has thin black cap, in summer black crest and chestnut frill. Juveniles have stripey heads.

GENERAL FEATURES

These are specialist waterbirds, coming to shore only to visit the nest on the water's edge. They are almost tailless, but have a long neck, smoothly curved head, and streamlined (but broad) body. The sexes are alike but the young are quite distinct, and all have a very different appearance in winter. The great crested is a large grebe, with striking pattern, crest and ruffs on head from late winter to autumn. The little grebe is the smallest and roundest. Divers are much larger and longer, with longer wings.

HABITAT

All breed on fresh water, but all can be seen on the sea in winter. The little grebe is more at home on small ponds and rivers.

Courtship
Find a lake with great crested grebes in February or March. Watch their courtship display and keep a diary of the way they behave. They will swim side by side, dive to pick up waterweed and bring it to the surface, face each other and wag their heads with their ruffs expanded, and quickly dip their heads down to peck at their backs. They chase off other grebes, and build their nests in reeds or flooded willows.

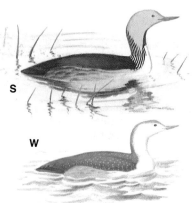

S

W

BLACK-THROATED DIVER
L 60cm. Grey head and white spots in oval patches on back in summer; straight bill.

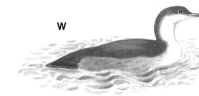

S

W

RED-THROATED DIVER
L 57cm. Brown back all year, red throat only in summer; slim, uptilted bill.

W

GREAT NORTHERN DIVER
L 80cm. Black head in summer; brown and white in winter, with dark collar.

S

W

S

RED-NECKED GREBE
L 45cm. Large black cap, white face, yellow on bill. Black and white in winter.

BLACK-NECKED GREBE
L 30cm. Uptilted bill, smudgy face, black and white. Gold ear tufts in summer.

LITTLE GREBE
L 25cm. Black head; face brownish-red in summer, grey in winter.

S

SEABIRDS

GENERAL FEATURES

Seabirds are varied. The gannet is closely related to the cormorant and shag, but it looks quite different from them. It shares features such as the structure of its bill, wings and feet (with all four toes joined by a broad web). But while young gannets are very dark, like cormorants, adults are mostly sparkling white and show up at long range.

HABITS

Cormorants and shags swim, and dive for fish from the surface. Gannets fly and dive in from the air, in dramatic, headlong plunges. Gannets swim on the sea but rarely perch, except at their colonies. Shearwaters and petrels come to land at night, and are best seen, flying over the sea, from a ship, or off a long headland.

Why cormorants stand with their wings stretched out is still argued about. They are probably drying feathers with no proper waterproofing, but the pose may help them digest a big meal of fish.

CORMORANT
L 90cm. Very big, with long head and bill. White thigh patches in spring.

juv

Continental race

W

SHAG
L 80cm. Snaky head with steep forehead, yellow patch, crest in spring. Young brown, white only on chin.

W S juv

STORM PETREL
L 15cm. Tiny black ocean bird; large white rump patch. Flutters low over waves.

GANNET
L 90cm. Huge white seabird, black wingtips; piebald young. Dives headlong for fish.

FULMAR
L 48cm. Stiff-winged, grey and white seabird; grey tail. Big white head, dark eyes.

MANX SHEARWATER
L 35cm. Black and white. Long wings; glides over the sea. Never found on cliffs in daytime.

PROJECT

Watch how seabirds dive into the water. For example, gannets plunge in very spectacularly, head-first with folded wings, from up to 30m or in a lower, slanting dive. They disappear deep underwater, often with a splash of spray.

HERONS AND BITTERNS

GENERAL HABITS

These elegant, long-necked waterside birds eat fish, newts, tadpoles and sometimes mice and voles – grey herons love eels. They fly with their necks hooked back in an S shape, and often stand like that, but they can stretch out their heads and use the long neck to stab forward in a lightning grab for a fish. The biggest enemy of a grey heron is frost: hard winters kill many of them, but after a few years the numbers build up again.

NESTING

Grey herons and egrets nest in trees, but purple herons and bitterns nest deep in thick reeds. They are best seen flying to and from the nest when they are busy feeding young. Herons at the nest are noisy and have many special courtship displays.

Grey herons nest in treetops, but even their giant nests are sometimes well hidden in weeping willows or leafy poplars. Purple herons' nests (above) are hidden carefully in dense reedbeds.

GREY HERON
L 95cm. Big, grey, with black and white head. Broad wings bowed in flight, with neck pulled in, legs trailing.

BITTERN ▷
L 75cm. Looks pale straw-buff. Broad, bowed wings, thick neck; deep booming call is unmistakable.

LITTLE BITTERN ⌂
L 35cm. Tiny, buff, brown and black, with pale wing patches. Flies fast over reedbeds.

juv

S

PURPLE HERON ⌂
L 80cm. Snaky head and neck, thin yellow bill; quite brown, with striped head.

LITTLE EGRET ⌂
L 55cm. Pure white; black legs, yellow feet, dark bill. Wades in shallow water.

HOW TO WATCH

Bitterns (right) are exceptionally difficult to see, keeping in dense reeds; little bitterns give themselves away by flying low above the reeds. Grey herons and egrets nest in treetops and you can watch from a distance (don't go too close – they are very nervous and will desert their eggs). Look for big stick nests with splashes of white droppings – a clue that they are in use and have young.

STORKS AND FLAMINGOS

WHITE STORK
L 100cm. Huge, black and white with red legs and bill, the stork is a familiar shape. In flight the legs trail back, the head is held straight out, the large wings are held flat.

GENERAL FEATURES

The remarkable flamingo has a 'bent' bill which it sweeps, upside-down, through water, like a sieve. The spoonbill has an equally odd bill; the flat, spatula-like tip swings sideways, partly open, through water, ready to snap shut on a fish. White storks have dagger-like bills, and snatch frogs, mice, large insects and fish.

HABITS

The flamingo and spoonbill are wading birds of marshes and salt lakes, but the stork is more of a marsh and meadowland bird, rarely going far into open water. Flocks of storks glide great distances on rising currents of warm air; flamingos fly in straggling lines, in big flocks.

White storks build huge nests of thick sticks (sparrows often nest in the bottom) and place them on rooftops of farms, church towers, even factory chimneys.

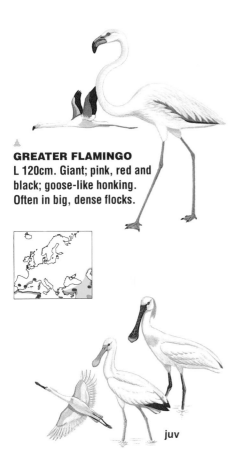

GREATER FLAMINGO
L 120cm. Giant; pink, red and black; goose-like honking. Often in big, dense flocks.

Watch these big birds feed. Storks are often found on grassy places, looking for grasshoppers, beetles and mice. They also feed in water, but still use their big beaks to grab or stab frogs and toads. The flamingo never stabs with its bill. It sweeps it 'upside-down' through water, which it sucks in then squirts out with its tongue; a fine mesh sieves out food – tiny water creatures – and keeps it inside to be swallowed. The spoonbill (below) sweeps its neck and head from side to side in shallow water.

juv

SPOONBILL
L 90cm. Big, white, with unique bill; swan-like flight. Young have pink bill.

juv

COMMON CRANE
L 110cm. Huge; elegant, slow; black and white head. Dark wingtips show in flight.

SWANS AND GEESE

MUTE SWAN
L 160cm. Orange and black bill (grey on young), with black knob. Bill points down.

GENERAL FEATURES

Swans are the easiest birds of all to find: they are so big, and pure white! But the wild swans – the Bewick's and whooper swans that come to western Europe each winter – are shy and difficult to get near, and not easy to tell apart.

HABITAT

In some places wild swans come regularly to the same area of floods, wet fields and lakes year after year, so are much more predictable. These places are often nature reserves; it is not so exciting as discovering your own wild swans while out birdwatching, but they do give better views, especially if there are hides to watch from. Mute swans are more tame and easy to see closely: just throw them some bread!

Mute swans point their bills downwards, curving their necks in a slight S shape. Whooper and Bewick's swans keep their heads and bills horizontal, with the neck straight and more upright, except when they are leaning forward to feed. Whoopers have longer necks.

BEWICK'S SWAN
L 120cm. Smaller; round yellow bill patch. Tail held low when swimming. Shy.

WHOOPER SWAN
L 150cm. Long, flat head; pointed yellow patch on bill. Shy; often on meadows.

juv

CANADA GOOSE
L 100cm. Black 'stocking' on neck, white chinstrap; brown body. Honks loudly. Flocks fly in V shapes.

PROJECT

Count the numbers of nesting swans in an area near your home each year (these are mute swans), and find out if they are increasing. Keep a diary of your observations. Also, see how many young they rear. Do they have good years and bad years? Do the pairs all have good numbers of cygnets in the same summer? Count the cygnets every week and see if all of them become full-grown. You may find that the family splits, some young staying with the male and some with the female.

GEESE

HABITS

Few groups of birds have such romantic and evocative associations as the geese. They arrive in autumn, often in large V-shaped flocks, moving south and making loud honking or gabbling calls that carry for miles. This is the sign of the winter to come; a few months later, as they head north, it is a sign of the coming spring at last.

FEEDING

Geese eat a lot of grass, and most farmers do not like them on their land. They live in flocks, feeding by grazing grass and marshland plants, or finding waste crops in fields. They need large areas of water to go to each night, where they are safe from foxes, and where they can drink and bathe. Families travel together during winter, and it is possible to count the numbers of young reared by each pair.

Flying flocks of geese, even when they are not going far, usually form long, diagonal lines or perfect V shapes in the sky. On migration, the older, stronger birds lead the way, while those at the back follow in the slipstream.

WHITE-FRONTED GOOSE
L 70cm. Grey-brown goose; adult has white blaze, black on belly. Young plainer. Bill usually pink with no black; legs vivid orange.

Eurasian race   Greenland race

PINK-FOOTED GOOSE ▼
L 70cm. Round, dark head, pale chest; black on bill. Back bluish-grey, with pale barring.

PROJECT

Wild geese are very wary and spot people a long way off, but the Canada goose is more approachable – this one is protecting its nest. You may find a car is a good hide. Find a flock of geese and look through them one by one: you will often find one or two 'odd ones out', such as a pink-footed goose in a flock of white-fronts.

BARNACLE GOOSE ▼
L 65cm. Black chest, white face; barred grey back. Barks. Flocks fly in lines or packs.

BEAN GOOSE ▼
L 80cm. Dark brown with very dark head, pale bars on back; long head and bill; orange legs.

GREYLAG GOOSE ▼
L 80cm. Large, heavy, pale; orange bill, pink legs. No black bars; noisy honks.

BRENT GOOSE ▼
L 58cm. Very dark; black head, neck and chest. Dark or (in north and west) whiter below. Deep croaking calls.

light-breasted

dark-breasted

DABBLING DUCKS

FOOD AND HABITAT

Birds of water and the water's edge, the dabbling, or surface-feeding, ducks eat plants, seeds, tiny water creatures and worms, which they sieve from water with their special, flat bills. Most can be seen on the coast as well as on fresh water but the garganey is usually on freshwater marshes. The shelduck feeds mostly on tiny snails sieved from estuarine mud.

Mallards nest early in spring and a duck with a dozen ducklings is a familiar sight. Sometimes ducks 'dump' eggs in other ducks' nests, and clutches far bigger than any one bird could lay can be found in one nest.

FLIGHT

All the ducks fly well and fast, but they are not very agile at speed, and tend to fly quite high and straight. To lose height, they 'whiffle' down, twisting from side to side in steep dives. They take off with a sudden leap from water or land (diving ducks have more of a pattering run across the surface). They are all quite at home on dry land, too, and walk well; the mallard will feed in fields far from water.

MALLARD
L 60cm. Colourful drake, brown duck; both have white-edged blue wing patch. Drake dark, browner in summer.

GADWALL
L 50cm. Dull grey or brown; black rear on male. White square on hindwing. Duck's bill orange at sides.

TEAL
L 35cm. Tiny, active; drake dark, head darker, white line on sides. Female brown with pale streak beside tail.

WIGEON
L 45cm. Drake pale, head darker; big white wing patch. Female brown; has short blue bill.

GARGANEY
L 40cm. Colourful drake; female has striped head. On shallow pools in summer.

PINTAIL
L 55cm. Long and slim; grey bill. Pale line along back of wing in flight. Pointed tail.

SHOVELER
L 50cm. Big bill; leans forward in water. Pale blue shoulders show in flight.

SHELDUCK
L 60cm. Goose-like; black and white. Vivid red bill, long pink legs; young duller.

DIVING DUCKS

GOOSANDER

L 65cm. Winter/spring male mostly pinky-white; summer male and female all year grey with rusty head. Female has clear-cut white chin (merganser's is blurred).

♂

♀

♂

FOOD AND FEEDING

They feed underwater, diving by ducking under from the surface as they swim (like grebes). The goosander is a fish-eater, with saw-like edges to its beak so it can grasp slippery prey more easily. The smew is similar – also a 'sawbill', as is the red-breasted merganser. The others eat shellfish, snails or water plants.

GENERAL HABITS

These ducks fly well, but take a short run to get airborne, and they go very fast but with little manoeuvrability – they need wide open spaces. On land they can hardly walk; their short legs are set far back and they stand quite upright (except for the horizontal goosander), and they are seen ashore much less often than the dabbling ducks. They don't quack, but have deep, growling calls.

Goosanders, goldeneyes and red-breasted mergansers are very much alike. But, while goosanders and goldeneyes nest in holes in trees, mergansers make a well-hidden nest in a grassy bank. Goosanders and goldeneyes will both use artificial nestboxes built specially for them.

POCHARD ▼
L 47cm. Sleepy diving duck; mostly grey with browner head; grey wing stripe.

TUFTED DUCK ▲
L 45cm. Active diving duck with white wing stripe. Crest long on male; female's short.

SMEW ▲
L 40cm. Male looks grey and white; female has neat white cheeks. Dives a lot.

GOLDENEYE ▲
L 45cm. Male mostly white; female very dark, round; white on wings. Always diving.

PROJECT

Watch pochards (below) and tufted ducks. The tufteds are lively, feeding during the day; pochards tend to feed at night and sleep by day. You will find that there will usually be more of one sex than the other. Is this always so? Is it the same for both species? Does the ratio of males to females vary from month to month? With goldeneyes you could see more adult males in early spring after they have spent the winter somewhere else – on gravel pits or reservoirs, or on the sea perhaps?

DIVING SEA DUCKS

HABITAT

Several diving ducks live on the sea in winter. The eider, common scoter and long-tailed duck rarely fly inland. The scaup is also a coastal bird, and the red-breasted merganser forms flocks on the sea in the late summer, after nesting near the coast (the goosander prefers fresh water).

Mergansers and shovelers have similar green-black heads, but their bills are very different. The merganser catches fish in its slender, hooked, saw-edged bill; the shoveler filters food in its broad, spoon-like bill.

HABITS

These birds are hardy and at home on the roughest water, floating like corks, and diving under to find their food. They tend to live in flocks, and fly about in long lines low over the water. Scoters are often far offshore and hard to see unless you can look out from a high cliff; then you may see a scattering of black dots a mile or two out in a big, sandy bay.

RED-BREASTED MERGANSER
L 60cm. Long and slender; winter male has big spiky crest (in summer like female). Female has smudgy face pattern.

COMMON SCOTER ▼
L 50cm. Male black with yellow bill spot; female has paler face; all-dark wings.

♂ W

♂ S

♀ W

♂

♀

LONG-TAILED DUCK ▲
L 45cm. Mostly white male has long tail; darker female has black cheek patch.

SCAUP ▷
L 45cm. Male has pale grey back. Female has broad white band around bill base.

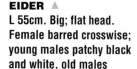

♀

♂

♀

♂

♂

VELVET SCOTER ▼
L 55cm. White on wing; female has two face spots.

EIDER ▲
L 55cm. Big; flat head. Female barred crosswise; young males patchy black and white, old males white on top.

♀

♂

HOW TO WATCH

Scaup like sheltered estuaries and bays, often near a sewage outfall or where grain or other food is tipped into the sea. Common scoters are often joined by velvet scoters, and these are best spotted when a flock takes flight. They also sit up and give one or two flaps of the wings – a good time to check the wing pattern. These are Eider ducks.

KITES AND HARRIERS

RED KITE
L 60cm. Long, forked red tail tilted in flight; white patch under wing. Buoyant flight, more supple than buzzard.

GENERAL FEATURES

Kites and harriers are long-winged, elegant birds of prey. They look quite slow in the air, but can fly rapidly when chasing prey. Kites have forked tails, but the fork is less easy to see when the tail is fully spread, and dark marsh harriers can be taken for black kites. But kites don't glide on raised wings, and harriers rarely fly with their wings angled down at the 'wrist', as kites do.

HABITS

Kites, but not harriers, feed at rubbish tips and scavenge for scraps; they also soar up high, using their superb eyesight to look for food. The harriers have long, slim legs – ideal for snatching small birds and mice from the long grass and reed stems over which they hunt.

Red kites are rare and often poisoned by mistake by baits put down to kill foxes. In Britain they are now found only in Wales, but a new scheme to bring them back to England and Scotland, by taking young birds from Sweden and Spain to safe areas, was started in 1989.

HEN HARRIER ▽
L 45cm. Male pale grey, rump white; female brown, rump white. Wings held up in V.

BLACK KITE ▲
L 56cm. Dark brown with pale band on upperwing; tail triangular with notch. Holds wings flat or bowed.

MONTAGU'S HARRIER ▽
L 43cm. Very slender; male grey, black bar across wing; female brown, white rump, long, pointed wingtips.

MARSH HARRIER ▲
L 55cm. Female dark with yellow on head; male grey and brown. Holds wings in V.

HOW TO WATCH

Watch for kites (this is a black kite) over farmland, village tips, wooded valley sides and upland moors. They circle like buzzards, often going high up, but keep their wings flat or even angled down at the tip. Harriers rarely fly so high (but do occasionally); they usually fly low over rough ground, and even when they soar they hold their wings up in a V.

OSPREY AND BUZZARDS

OSPREY
L 55cm. Large, long-winged, short-tailed; very white underneath. White head with dark band; wings are 'kinked' at wrist.

GENERAL FEATURES

The buzzard is quite common in many areas, and often perches on wires or telegraph poles, something an eagle would never do! If a bird looks beautifully patterned underneath with cream, gold and brown, circles overhead in a wooded valley, and calls with a loud, piercing sound, it is a buzzard (golden eagles like high, craggy mountains and wild moors and rarely come close to people).

HABITS

Rough-legged buzzards are rare winter birds in much of Europe. The osprey is a summer visitor, spending winter in Africa; it is unique in its habit of diving for fish, a really thrilling sight. The honey buzzard is a migrant, flying across the Mediterranean in large flocks, but spreading thinly over most of Europe to nest; it eats grubs and wax from bee and wasp nests.

Ospreys dive for fish, going head-first until they near the water, then swinging their legs forward and hitting the water feet-first. Fish are grabbed in the feet and carried off to a perch, or to the nest, which is usually at the top of a large tree.

BUZZARD

L 55cm. Mostly brown; some much paler. Shorter wings and tail than eagle's. Usually low over woods.

dark

paler

PROJECT

If you live in, or go on holiday to, a good buzzard area – Wales, the English Lake District, or southern France – the best time to see buzzards is early spring. Choose a fine, sunny morning and find a vantage point in a wooded valley. The buzzards will circle above their nesting territories for hours.

HONEY BUZZARD

L 57cm. Large, with long, three-barred tail; wings drooped; narrow head sticks out like cuckoo's.

♂

ROUGH-LEGGED BUZZARD

L 60cm. Big; white tail with black band; often hovers. Longer wings than buzzard's.

GOLDEN EAGLE ▷

L 90cm. Very large; often very high over peaks. Dark (young have white patches).

61

HAWK AND FALCONS

PEREGRINE
L 45cm. Large, blue-grey
falcon with black head, white
neck. 'Anchor shape' in air.
Quick, stiff wingbeats, with
short glides.

GENERAL FEATURES

These dashing birds of prey form two groups –
the falcons, with round heads sunk into
hunched shoulders, short legs and long, pointed
wings; and the hawks, with flatter heads, a
more alert look, and shorter, broader, blunt
wings designed for fast, twisting flight between
trees. All have hooked bills (the falcons have a
notch or 'tooth') and sharp claws or talons for
grasping prey.

HABITS

Prey is caught in the feet, then killed with the
bill. Falcons like open areas, but spend a lot of
time perched. They soar and glide well, and
catch prey after a fast, dashing chase. The
kestrel hovers, as if it hangs from a string.
Hawks fly low when hunting, speeding up to
take birds by surprise.

The flight of a peregrine is
marvellous, especially when
it is hunting or displaying.
After circling at a great
height it will close its wings
and plunge headlong in a
stoop, stopping abruptly to
land on a rock ledge.

SPARROWHAWK

L 35cm. Broad-based wings, blunt at tip; long tail. Quick flaps between glides.

GOSHAWK

L 55cm. Very big; like long-tailed buzzard or giant sparrowhawk with longer wings and bigger, longer head.

MERLIN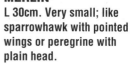

L 30cm. Very small; like sparrowhawk with pointed wings or peregrine with plain head.

HOBBY

L 35cm. Slim, long-winged, with short tail. Elegant flight, swooping for insects.

KESTREL

L 35cm. Common; hovers as if hanging on string. Male blue-grey on head and tail.

PROJECT

If you travel over the same route by car, bus or train regularly, make a weekly kestrel count. They are easy to see, sitting on wires or poles (often beside a road) or hovering in the air with flickering wings, staring at the ground in search of voles. Do you see more after the nesting season?

GROUSE

GENERAL FEATURES

Grouse are rounded, hunch-backed, short-legged birds, rather like chickens with feathered feet. Red grouse are dark brown, closely speckled with buff, the males redder than the hens. Male black grouse have unique curved tail feathers and broad white wingbars, but hens are like rather large, pale red grouse. Capercaillies are huge woodland birds, the males almost turkey-like.

HABITS AND HABITAT

Capercaillies prefer trees and dense vegetation in pine woods, and black grouse like woodland edges and moors with scattered bushes and copses. Even red grouse feed in hawthorn bushes sometimes, but they prefer open heather moors. Ptarmigan are mountain-top birds, living up near the snowline.

Capercaillie display
Capercaillies have a wonderful display. The male fans out his stiff, waxy tail feathers, stretches up his head and puffs out a rough, spiky 'beard'. He then struts around making a very strange mixture of rattles, croaks and burps, with some noises just like the sound of a cork popping from a bottle. Other males are chased off, or fight in a flurry of wings.

CAPERCAILLIE
L 60–90cm. Male very big, dark grey and brown; hen smaller, bright rusty-brown.

RED GROUSE

L 35cm. Crouches in heather, flies up with loud clatter; dark red-brown.

♂ S

♂ S

♂ W

♂ W

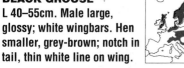

♀

♂

BLACK GROUSE

L 40–55cm. Male large, glossy; white wingbars. Hen smaller, grey-brown; notch in tail, thin white line on wing.

PTARMIGAN

L 35cm. White, or grey-brown with white wings; high up around snow line. Croaks.

♂

♀

HAZEL HEN

L 45cm. Brown and grey; broad, rounded tail with black band. Found in forest.

♀

♂

HOW TO WATCH

Black grouse are quite rare and must be searched for with care in moorland areas with scattered trees and patches of woodland. The males display at a traditional 'lek', making loud, bubbling, coos and wheezy sneezing sounds as they spread their unique, curved tails and have mock fights. These leks must not be disturbed; if you know of one it is important to keep well hidden – and be there by dawn for the best view!

PHEASANT AND PARTRIDGES

PHEASANT
L 60–90cm. Female brown; pointed tail. Colourful male large; dark green and red head, some with neck ring.

HABITS

Pheasants and partridges are ground-living birds. The pheasant likes woods, though, and will roost in trees; it is also fond of wet reedbeds. It often flies up at the last moment, with a scary rush and clatter of wings, when disturbed in a wood. Partridges like much more open places such as meadows and cereal fields. Red-leggeds prefer to run rather than fly, even if surprised just a few metres away. They sometimes perch on top of walls and haystacks in spring, calling their strange, chuffing-steam-engine-like noises and a 'chuk-chuk-chuc-ar'.

THE ELUSIVE QUAIL

The quail is a bit of a mystery bird, sometimes found in many cereal fields but in most years elusive. It keeps well hidden and most people never see one, just hearing calls at dusk.

Pheasants are reared for shooting and gamekeepers will not be pleased if you trespass near the rearing pens. In autumn it is safest to keep well away from the rearing wood in case a shoot is about to begin nearby.

flight
from
rear

QUAIL

L 18cm. Tiny, secretive in long crops; bright, quick call 'whit whit-it' best clue.

♂

juv

flight

♀

flight from rear

GREY PARTRIDGE ▷

L 30cm. Rounded, pale brown, streaked; orange face and dark mark on breast. Call creaky 'kirr-ik' from meadow.

RED-LEGGED PARTRIDGE

L 35cm. Large, round; plain brown with barred sides, white face edged with black specks.

♂

♀

HOW TO WATCH

A good view over farmland in spring will often give the best chance of seeing pheasants. The handsome cock birds (above right) walk about in the open, especially in the evenings. Partridges call early in the morning and late in the day, too – grey partridges (below right) mostly from flowery hay meadows or cattle pastures. Quails prefer rolling fields of wheat, or large hayfields, on chalk downs. Dusk and dawn are the best times to listen for their quick, liquid, rhythmic calls, but tracking them down is extremely difficult.

MOORHEN AND COOT

GENERAL FEATURES

These are fascinating birds. They are subtly but beautifully marked (except for the plain, black coot), with shiny, richly coloured feathers.

HABITAT AND HABITS

Crakes and rails, including the common moorhen and coot, inhabit watersides and wet places, apart from the corncrake, which lives in hayfields and damp, grassy places. Coots like open water, from the park lake up to big reservoirs (even, sometimes, the sea), and also feed on short grass nearby; they are often in big flocks, up to hundreds at a time. Moorhens go about in twos and threes or a dozen or so, and like riversides, ditches, tiny ponds and wet fields alongside such watery places. The water rail is much harder to see, living in dense reeds, rushes and among flooded willows; it makes loud, pig-like squeals and grunts.

By late spring, moorhens have full-grown young and sometimes lay a second set of eggs. Watch the family. When the new chicks hatch, the older ones from the first nest sometimes help their parents to feed them – a remarkable piece of family behaviour.

MOORHEN
L 33cm. Nervous, shy, with bobbing head, jerked tail. Tail cocked to show white below; white line along body.

juv

Coots dive for food much more than moorhens. They are like tufted ducks in the way they swim about on the surface and duck under, but they seem much more buoyant, popping back up like corks, and sometimes even bouncing up out of the water tail-first! Watch them dive and try to single out one bird. Then time its dives with a stopwatch or a wristwatch. Compare the coots' dives with those of tufted ducks and grebes, then compare them in different pools. Get some idea of the depth of the water if you can: do the times differ in different depths?

WATER RAIL ▽
L 28cm. Rounded from side; thin, flattened end-on. Red bill; barred sides; buff rear.

◁ **CORNCRAKE**
L 27cm. Very rare. In hay and iris beds, secretive; loud call, harsh 'crek-crek'.

COOT ▷
L 38cm. Big and rounded; tail held low down, not cocked; no white on body but large white facial shield.

WADERS

GENERAL FEATURES

Oystercatchers are big, black and white waders, easy to identify. Avocets and stilts are also large, with distinctive bills, while stone-curlews are shy, well-camouflaged birds. The phalaropes are tiny, grey and white in winter but brightly coloured in summer.

HABITS AND HABITAT

Oystercatchers are very noisy, giving loud, fast piping displays with bowed heads; they spend the winter on estuaries and mussel beds, but in summer like quiet beaches and stony riversides. Avocets need shallow water and very wet mud; they feed by sweeping their bills sideways through the surface. Stilts are Mediterranean birds. Stone-curlews like hot sandy places, but also heaths and stony fields farther north; they never feed on the shore. The phalaropes are ocean birds in winter, but they nest around remote lakes; they swim like tiny ducks, and spin like tops to stir up food.

Oystercatchers with pointed bills prise shellfish off rocks and slide the bill inside to cut the muscle that closes the shell. Those with square-tipped bills chisel shells open. The tips of both are often worn down.

OYSTERCATCHER
L 43cm. Black and white; young birds browner on back. In winter, bill may have dark tip; white around throat.

AVOCET
L 43cm. Mostly frosty white; long grey legs. Bill uniquely curved upwards.

STONE-CURLEW
L 40cm. Large, pale brown; pale base to bill and white on face show up best, then bar across wing, yellow legs.

BLACK-WINGED STILT
L 40cm. Very long pink legs and needle-like bill; young are brown above at first.

RED-NECKED PHALAROPE
L 17cm. Round body; very fine bill. Dark grey and white in winter, black mask. Swims.

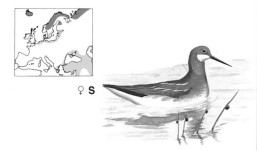

♀ S

GREY PHALAROPE
L 19cm. Bill yellow at base; pale grey and white in winter. Swims like a cork out at sea.

♀ S

PROJECT

Watch these waders feed. How do they reach food in water and on mud? Avocets' delicate bills (below) sweep sideways to find food by touch. Stilts wade in very deep with their long legs, but pick insects from the water surface with their fine bills. They may also snatch fish fry, but, like avocets, they never probe or hammer.

PLOVERS

juv

GENERAL FEATURES

Although called wading birds, plovers prefer to
keep their feet dry, whether on the sand or
mud at the edge of a lake or the sea, or on
moors and fields. The grey, ringed and little
ringed are beach birds (the little ringed by fresh
water), but the golden prefers moors in summer
and grassland or ploughed fields outside the
nesting season. They have quite long legs, but
short bills for picking, not probing.

HABITS

Plovers have a distinctive 'run-stop-tilt' forward-
run action as they feed, dashing a little way to
snatch up a worm or insect, then pausing to
look for more. They fly fast on their sharp-
pointed wings.

A plover with eggs or chicks
will slip away from them,
then attract your attention to
try to lead you away from the
nest. It flops down, spreads
one wing and its tail, and
calls loudly, looking as if it
really has a broken wing!

KENTISH PLOVER
L 17cm. Small and pale;
male with black, female
brown, mark beside neck.
Black legs.

GREY PLOVER
L 30cm. Mottled grey; looks
dark at long range. Black
armpits, white rump in flight;
'teeyoo-ee' whistle.

LITTLE RINGED PLOVER
L 14cm. Black bill, yellow
ring around eye; no wingbar;
sharp 'pew' call. Not winter.

GOLDEN PLOVER
L 28cm. Mottled yellow;
brown at long range. White
armpits, dark rump in flight.

HOW TO WATCH

Wader flocks often include ringed
plovers, which forage over
mudflats at low tide. Grey plovers
do the same on the larger
estuaries. Look for flocks of
golden plovers (often with
lapwings) on grassy fields and
ploughed corn stubbles, or on
upland moors or heathlands
when breeding (right). They look
sharp-winged in flight compared
with blunt-winged lapwings.

LAPWING AND SNIPE

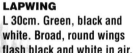

LAPWING
L 30cm. Green, black and
white. Broad, round wings
flash black and white in air.

GENERAL FEATURES

Lapwings are plovers, but quite unlike the
brown and white ringed plovers, or the
spangled-backed grey and golden plovers. Snipe
and woodcock are beautifully camouflaged in
black, brown and cream colours.

HABITS

Lapwings breed on damp fields (and are
declining as so many places are drained) and
spend the winter on marshes, ploughed fields
and wet meadows. Snipe like similar places, but
need spots with soft mud where they can probe
deeply for worms. Jack snipe breed in
Scandinavia but move south for the winter,
living in dense sedge and grass with water
underfoot. Woodcocks are woodland birds,
nesting and feeding in the leaf mould; on
summer nights they fly regular circuits
over their woods.

Lapwings are very noisy on
their nesting grounds. Try not
to disturb them. If you or a
fox do, or even if a passing
sheep does so, they will fly
around calling hysterically
with loud, mournful 'pee-
weet' calls until the intruder
moves away.

WOODCOCK
L 35cm. Woodland edge.
Heavy; bars on back of head.
Flies at dusk over treetops.

JACK SNIPE
L 19cm. Small; quiet, very
secretive. Fluttery flight for
short distance, then drops.

SNIPE
L 27cm. Long bill; hides in
marsh. Stripes of cream on
head, back. Zigzag flight.

HOW TO WATCH

Snipe (right) nest in wet meadows
and on damp moors. Find them by
listening for their rhythmic 'chip-
per' calls and their drumming
displays. They dive through the air
with outspread tail feathers, which
vibrate and make a whirring,
trembling sound (below).

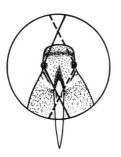

Woodcocks (left) probe for worms
in soft leaf litter and damp ground.
They have flexible bill-tips that feel
and grasp worms underground.
While probing, they risk being
caught: but they have eyes set so
far back that they can see behind
them as well as in front!

SMALL WADERS

DUNLIN
L 18cm. Slightly dumpy, hunched; bill usually drooped. Black belly in summer only.

S

W

GENERAL HABITS

Small waders congregate at the water's edge. In winter, an estuary is the place to go to see hundreds of them. They spread out to feed on wet mud and sand as the tide falls, but come together again in large, tightly-packed flocks to rest at high tide; a wader roost has birds jostling shoulder to shoulder for two or three hours. Knots even feed in close flocks, but dunlins spread more widely, and sanderlings scamper about on sand near the waves. Turnstones and purple sandpipers prefer rockier places, feeding among seaweed and barnacles.

ARCTIC TRAVELLERS

Little stints and curlew sandpipers breed in the Arctic and are likely to be seen only in spring and autumn, often with migrating dunlins near muddy reservoirs inland.

Waders breed in the north and go south for the winter, so in spring and autumn they undertake huge journeys. On their way they stop off to feed in muddy or sandy spots near water, so you can often find sandpipers – this is a wood sandpiper – dunlins, ruffs and greenshanks by lakes, reservoirs and gravel pits in April and May and again from August to October.

Sp

CURLEW SANDPIPER
L 20cm. Like pale, elegant dunlin with longer legs and bill, white rump. Red in spring only; peachy in the autumn.

W

W

TURNSTONE ▲
L 23cm. Chunky, heavy; short orange legs; thick bill slightly upturned. In winter very dark with white marks.

KNOT ▷
L 25cm. Dumpy, middle-sized; grey in winter with pale grey rump; short legs. Often in big 'smoky' flocks.

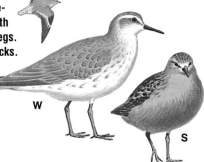

W

S

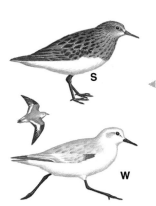

LITTLE STINT ▽
L 15cm. Tiny; very white below; black legs and short black bill. Pale V on back. Quick, short run over mud.

juv

PURPLE SANDPIPER ▲
L 22cm. Dark; white around eye and underneath; legs dull orange-yellow. Likes rocky headlands, seaweed.

S

SANDERLING ◁
L 20cm. Very pale grey and white in winter; black legs, straight black bill; quick.

W

RUFF, GODWITS AND CURLEWS

GENERAL FEATURES

Long bills are essential for probing deep into mud for worms, but long legs are not needed by birds that feed mostly out of the water on muddy beaches. The curlew and whimbrel, whose bills bend down, are not very long-legged; they breed on dry moors. The black-tailed godwit nests in wet pastures; its bill and legs are longer than the bar-tailed's, whose bill curves upwards slightly. Both winter on estuaries. The ruff has longish legs for wading but a medium-length bill for picking food off the mud surface.

HABITS

Curlews and godwits are waterside birds outside the breeding season, roosting in flocks at high tide. The ruff prefers freshwater pools and marshes.

Ruffs (above) and black-tailed godwits nest inland, on wet meadows that often flood in winter but are grazed by cattle in spring. Such places are now rare, as most wet fields have been drained, so these birds are rare, too. The best places are still in the Netherlands, but even there they have declined dramatically.

RUFF
L 22–30cm. Male in spring has coloured ruff, soon lost in summer. Red legs. Autumn birds very neat; legs ochre, bill short; long neck.

BLACK-TAILED GODWIT
L 40cm. Tall, long-billed and large; broad white wing stripes. Grey in winter, dark coppery-red in spring.

W

S

BAR-TAILED GODWIT
L 38cm. Bill faintly upcurved. No wingbars. Brown in winter, deep red in spring.

W

S

CURLEW
L 60cm. Very big, streaky brown; long, evenly curved bill; 'cur-lee' call.

WHIMBREL
L 40cm. Big, dark; striped head; bill kinked down; high, fast 'ti-ti-ti-ti-ti' call. Spring and autumn.

PROJECT

Curlews (right) and godwits have very long bills. These large waders feed on soft mud, probing deeply for lugworms, but curlews also eat crabs, and earthworms in meadows. Watch godwits feed: how many of their probes are successful? Do they catch more worms by the tideline or on drier mud? Do they catch more in a flock, or when they are on their own?

LARGER SANDPIPERS

GENERAL FEATURES

The large sandpipers and 'shanks' are middle-sized waders, all much smaller than the godwits. They have quite long legs but medium-length bills.

HABITAT

These birds like fresh water, but the redshank is also common on the seashore. Green sandpipers like small ditches and ponds, where they often stay the winter. Wood sandpipers are seen in spring and autumn, beside freshwater pools with muddy shores. Spotted redshanks are seen mostly in autumn (black ones in spring are rare), usually in coastal marshes. Common sandpipers are summer visitors to upland rivers, but you will find them by lakes and reservoirs in autumn, even in lowland areas.

Greenshanks are very active, and sometimes dash about in shallow water (or even to above their legs) trying to catch tiny fish. They seem to stir the fish up with their feet, even lunge for them with their bills. Spotted redshanks do the same, but often even more quickly and in groups.

GREENSHANK
L 30cm. Tall and elegant, but often leans forward. Grey-green legs; slightly uptilted bill. No wingbars.

W

REDSHANK ▷
L 27cm. Brown, dark; broad white bands on wings. Loud, quick 'tchu-yu-yu' calls.

S

SPOTTED REDSHANK
L 30cm. Usually very pale; long red legs, straight black bill. No wingbars. 'Chewit'.

WOOD SANDPIPER ◁
L 20cm. Neat; brown with pale spots, line over eye. White above tail, dull wings.

GREEN SANDPIPER ▲
L 22cm. Looks black-and-white, especially in flight; black underwings; dark above, with large square white patch.

PROJECT

Redshanks are seen on estuaries in winter, but try to find a wet freshwater marsh where they nest. In spring they fly around and settle with raised wings, showing off the white, while calling very loudly. They often sit on high posts.

COMMON SANDPIPER ▲
L 20cm. Brown and white; swings long tail up and down as it walks; stiff flight. White wingbars obvious.

TERNS

ARCTIC TERN
L 35cm. Round head; short bill all dark red, tiny legs. Clean, pale upperwing. Very white underwing, all see-through from beneath.

GENERAL FEATURES

Most terns are silvery-grey and white, but they have neat, jet-black caps in summer. The black is partly lost in autumn and winter, when the forehead is white. The little tern has a white forehead all year.

HABITS

Terns often hover over water, as if hanging on a string, and then dive head-first to catch a fish. The black tern is more of an insect-eater, and swoops to pick food from the water's surface. It is also mostly a freshwater tern, while the others are often known as 'sea terns'. This is not a strict rule, though, as all species can appear at a lake or reservoir on spring and autumn migration.

Terns however, are smaller than gulls, more slender, with long tails. Gulls are broader-winged and squarer-tailed than terns. The herring gull is the typical seagull, pale grey and white.

COMMON TERN ▷
L 33cm. Slim; pale grey, whiter below, black cap; orange-red bill has black tip.

BLACK TERN ▷
L 25cm. Black with white below tail in spring; dark grey and white in autumn, dark chest spot each side.

ROSEATE TERN ▽
L 38cm. Big; very long-tailed with black bill and red legs. Very white.

LITTLE TERN ▽
L 25cm. Tiny; whirring wingbeats; yellow bill and legs. Pure white below.

SANDWICH TERN △
L 40cm. Big; short-tailed with black bill and legs. Very pale; grating 'kier-ink' call note.

PROJECT

Roseate terns (right) are very rare birds. Many were killed for fun by children in Africa, so a new wildlife club was set up in Ghana and many children now belong to it, and don't kill birds. If you would like a penfriend in Ghana, write to the RSPB (International), Sandy, Beds, SG19 2DL. Watch terns in the late summer and autumn. Even on migration young birds call to their parents to be fed. They have browner marks on their wings, and darker bills. You can easily spot them.

GULLS AND SKUAS

GULLS

Gulls are common, and often taken for granted, but few birds are more beautiful and few fly better than the agile 'seagulls' that we all know so well. Whether they are following a plough inland, flying behind a cross-Channel ferry, or stealing sandwiches on the seafront, they are nimble, acrobatic and powerful in the air. The kittiwake is a special one, as it spends most of its life out at sea – a real sea gull – while the others are much happier around the tideline or on land.

SKUAS

Skuas are like dark, fast-flying gulls with long, supple wings. They catch fish, and kill smaller birds, too, but their special feature is food-piracy: they chase other birds until they cough up food, which the skuas then eat!

Gulls
Rubbish tips are not very pleasant places, but they are good for gulls in winter. Find a viewpoint off the tip and in a safe place, and watch the gulls from a distance. You may find some of the scarcer species coming to scavenge from the refuse, along with spectacular flocks of the commoner ones. Count the number of young ones every month: does the proportion change in spring?

BLACK-HEADED GULL
L 36cm. Small, very pale; in summer, dark head, dark red bill and legs. In winter, whiter head, brighter red bill and legs.

ARCTIC SKUA

L 45cm. Tail spike; dark, or with white belly. Pale wing flash often seen.

dark adult

juv

pale adult

GREAT BLACK-BACKED GULL

L 65cm. Huge. Blackest back; pale pink legs. Young ones boldy chequered brown.

COMMON GULL

L 40cm. Neat, slim; mid-grey back, green legs, greeny bill with no red. Dark eye.

2 years old

LESSER BLACK-BACKED GULL

L 55cm. Big; back dark grey, legs yellow. Young ones very dark brown, bill black.

GREAT SKUA

L 60cm. Very big, heavy; brown with big white wing patches.

2 years old

KITTIWAKE

L 38cm. Neat black wingtip triangles; black legs; usually out at sea or on cliffs.

HERRING GULL

L 58cm. Big, pale; legs pink, eye pale. Streaky head in winter. Young pale brown.

AUKS

PUFFIN
L 30cm. Tubby, short legs;
big triangular bill (smaller,
dull in winter), pale face.
On grassy slopes.

juv

HABITAT

Some of the most numerous seabirds of the
North Atlantic, the North Sea and the oceans
of the far north are the auks. These include the
guillemot, razorbill and puffin, all of which nest
in huge colonies on sea cliffs and islands. The
black guillemot is far less common, and prefers
little rocky islets and sheltered bays or
harbours.

DANGERS

Because of oil spills from shipwrecked tankers,
fishing nets (which catch hundreds of
thousands of birds as well as fish) and
overfishing (which deprives them of food), these
birds have become much scarcer in places. But
their colonies, often with kittiwakes, still
provide some of the most thrilling and
spectacular birdwatching in Europe.

Seabird cliffs ▷
Seabirds nesting on a cliff
look chaotic but have a
regular order. Puffins,
gulls (1) and fulmars like
the very top. Gannets (2)
prefer broad ledges,
guillemots (3) narrow ledges
high up; razorbills (4) nest in
hollows among the
guillemots. Kittiwakes (5)
are on tiny ledges lower
down, where shags take over
the bigger shelves of rock.
Cormorants (6) may be down
with the shags, or up near
the top where ledges are
relatively wider.

BLACK GUILLEMOT
L 35cm. Sooty, with white ovals on wings. Mostly white with black bars on top in winter. Red legs.

juv

S

W

LITTLE GULL
L 27cm. Small, tern-like but rounder wings; W across wings of young birds; underwing black, edged white, on adults.

W

S

GUILLEMOT
L 42cm. Pointed bill, square tail. Browner head. Pale face with dark eyestripe in winter.

HOW TO WATCH

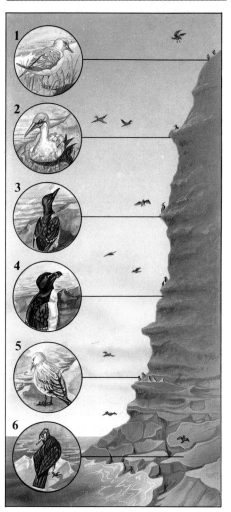

W

RAZORBILL
L 40cm. Square bill, pointed tail. Black head with white stripes; black down to eye in winter.

CUCKOO, PIGEONS AND DOVES

CUCKOO
L 34cm. Slender, grey with white tail spots. Wings broad but taper to swept-back point. Yellow on bill and yellow eye.

GENERAL FEATURES

Pigeons and doves – the two words are almost interchangeable – are soft-plumaged, rounded, medium-sized birds, with small round heads, rather long wings and tails and short legs. The cuckoo is much slimmer and longer-tailed, with a thinner, more pointed head shape as it flies. Cuckoos also perch with their wings drooped, and cock the tail and wave it from side to side.

HABITS

Doves and pigeons feed on the ground, but cuckoos fly down to pick food from the ground and take it back to a perch, rarely walking far. Woodpigeons form huge flocks, often mixed with stock doves; stock doves also make smaller flocks on their own. The turtle dove is the only migrant dove, going to Africa in winter, like the cuckoo.

Cuckoos arrive in mid April and sing until June or July. The male makes the 'cuck-oo' call and the female has a loud, beautiful, bubbling voice. They also have a harsh, wheezy laughing call. Young cuckoos are hatched and then fed by other birds.

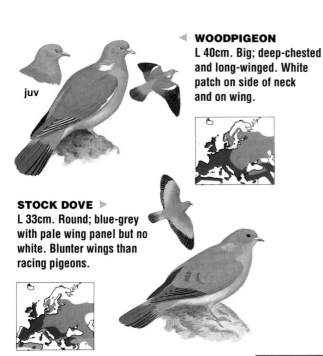

juv

WOODPIGEON
L 40cm. Big; deep-chested and long-winged. White patch on side of neck and on wing.

juv

TURTLE DOVE ◢
L 28cm. Small, neat; spots on brown back; white V on tail shows on take-off or landing. Bluish on wing; purring call. Summer.

STOCK DOVE ▷
L 33cm. Round; blue-grey with pale wing panel but no white. Blunter wings than racing pigeons.

ROCK DOVE ▽
L 34cm. Rare, on remote cliffs; broad white patch on back. Like clean town pigeon.

COLLARED DOVE ▷
L 30cm. Common all year; pale pinky-grey, black ring on neck. Pale under tail-tip. Loud 'cu-coo-cuk' all day.

OWLS AND NIGHTJAR

TAWNY OWL
L 38cm. Large, rich brown.
Black eyes. Makes wonderful
hooting calls and a sharper
'kewick'.

GENERAL FEATURES

Owls are thick-set, rounded birds with large,
flat or rounded heads and short legs. Those
that perch in trees tend to sit upright, with
their tails below the perch, but those that stand
on the ground have a more sloping stance. The
barn owl is unusual, being so beautifully pale,
but even the darker tawny owl can look white
in car headlights. The slimmer nightjar is not
an owl, but does fly at night.

HABITAT

Tawny owls are woodland birds, also found in
parks with plenty of big evergreens. Little owls
like farms and also coastal cliffs. Short-eared
prefer open moorland and marshes, while long-
eareds nest in woods and copses or dense
thickets of hawthorn and willow. The nightjar
catches moths in flight over heaths.

Owls regurgitate indigestible
bits of food as pellets. You
can find pellets under trees,
or in old barns. Soak them
and carefully pull them apart
with tweezers. You will find
jawbones, skulls and other
parts of mice and voles,
beetle wing-cases and other
items that show you what the
owl has eaten.

BARN OWL ▷
L 35cm. Large head with white face; all-white below except on Continent. Bars along wings show in flight.

LITTLE OWL ▽
L 22cm. Fierce face, yellow eyes; dumpy, but bobs and stretches comically. Flight bounds up and down.

SHORT-EARED OWL ▽
L 38cm. Pale brown with brown and buff 'wrist' marks; belly unstreaked white.

LONG-EARED OWL ▽
L 36cm. Slim but big; 'horns' raised in alarm. Streaks; orange patch on wing.

NIGHTJAR ▽
L 26cm. Midsummer nights, over heaths; long wings and tail; vibrant purring song.

HOW TO WATCH

Owls are difficult to watch because most come out at night. The tawny (right) and long-eared are least likely to be seen by day and must be looked for at the edge of a wood as it gets dark: listen for their strange calls. Try to find short-eared owls in winter, over a reedbed or coastal marshes; you can watch them in the afternoon before it gets too dark.

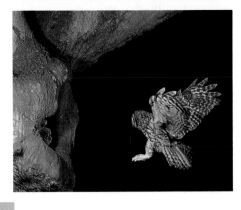

SWIFTS AND KINGFISHER

KINGFISHER
L 16cm. Flash of electric-blue on back; orange below. Small and hard to spot.

GENERAL FEATURES

Swifts are splendid birds of the air, perfect for flying; so much so that they cannot perch. You will never see them on wires like swallows. They have extremely long, stiff, blade-like wings. The kingfisher is stumpy-tailed, with a very large head and bill and tiny legs. Bee-eaters are like 'stretched' starlings with longer bodies and wings and elegant gliding flight. The hoopoe flies in swooping bounds on broad wings. On the ground it waddles on short legs like a pigeon, hard to spot.

HABITS

Swifts fly high up in groups. The kingfisher is always by clear water; bee-eaters sit on wires or twigs and fly up after insects.

Kingfishers need a steep sandy bank above water to nest in. They dive at the bank, scratching a hollow with beak and feet, then dig a long, narrow tunnel; this soon becomes lined with fish bones.

ROLLER
L 30cm. Green-blue and brown; flashes vivid blues when flying down to insect on ground.

display flight

BEE-EATER
L 28cm. Unique; pointed tail, long triangular wings. Rich, ringing 'prrup' call gives away birds overhead.

SWIFT
L 17cm. Very dark; scythe-like wings, forked tail, very short head. Screeching call.

ALPINE SWIFT
L 22cm. Big swift with pale brown back, white belly and chin. Very rare in UK.

HOOPOE
L 28cm. Unique; dazzling black and white bars; fan-like crest. Hard to see on ground.

juv

PROJECT

Despite their colours, kingfishers are not easy to see. Walk slowly, quietly, beside rivers and gravel pits. Look along overhanging bushes; listen for shrill 'chi-kee' whistles as they fly, and 'plops' as they dive in. If you spot one, keep very still. Watch carefully and study the success of its dives for fish: does the kingfisher get a fish every dive, every second dive, or what?

WOODPECKERS

GENERAL HABITS

Few birds are so specialised as these – they are rarely seen away from the trees they need to supply their food and nest sites. Green woodpeckers actually feed on the ground a lot, searching for insects, but if disturbed fly to hide in a tree, often perching behind the trunk and peeping around. Lesser spotteds flutter about in the tops of tall trees, but come lower in winter, and great spotteds are usually seen in large trees (but occasionally move into hedgerows and visit birdtables).

A green woodpecker's tongue is long and sticky, with a barbed point. It probes into anthills and the ants are dragged out and swallowed. When not being used, the tongue winds back, like a coiled spring, into a groove under the top of the woodpecker's skull!

A SUMMER VISITOR

Wrynecks differ from woodpeckers, being summer visitors. They feed on ants and do not have the same strong, chisel-like bill that other woodpeckers have.

juv

GREEN WOODPECKER
L 32cm. Large; green with yellow on back. Red cap. Laughing call. Young birds barred dark green.

♂

◁ **BLACK WOODPECKER**
L 45cm. Very big; black with red cap (male) or patch on back of head (female). Loud, machine-gun drumming.

♂

Look for woodpecker nest holes in trees – neat, round ones for great spotteds (below), much bigger, more egg-shaped for blacks. Notice woodpecker damage to old and dead trees, with bark pecked away, chips out of dead wood. Black woodpeckers chip pieces from logs on ground. Green woodpeckers dig into anthills, leaving tell-tale holes and scrapes, and curled white-ended droppings. Listen for drumming in spring – loud, sudden, abrupt drum-rolls on resonant wood. It is possible, with experience, to identify woodpeckers by their drumming.

LESSER SPOTTED WOODPECKER ▷
L 15cm. Tiny, barred; red cap on male. High, squeaky 'pee-pee-pee-pee' call.

♀

♂

GREAT SPOTTED WOODPECKER ▽
L 23cm. Striking red under tail. White shoulder patches. Loud 'tchik' call.

♂

juv

WRYNECK ▷
L 15cm. Secretive, elusive; beautifully marked. Bars on tail, dark stripe down neck. Nasal 'kyeu-kyeu-kyeu'.

LARKS AND PIPITS

SKYLARK
L 18cm. Streaky brown; slight crest; streaks on breast end in sharp band. White outer tail feathers.

GENERAL FEATURES

Larks and pipits look quite similar but are not really closely related. The pipits are more like the wagtails, in fact, and have the same rather sleek, long-tailed look (but their bodies are really quite rounded); they also have spindly legs and very thin bills. Larks are chunkier in shape, deep-chested, with shorter legs and thicker bills.

HABITS

Some pipits are summer visitors, others move around a lot: the meadow is in Britain all year but goes to the hills in summer, lowlands in spring and autumn, and often to the coast in winter. Water pipits breed on European mountains but move low down in winter, a few even going to England and Wales. Skylarks visit western Europe in winter in large flocks, from farther east; the skylarks that nest in western Europe tend to keep apart, in smaller groups or families.

Watch skylarks in spring and early summer and you cannot fail to wonder how they sing for so long, non-stop, while working so hard to keep hovering in the air. Why not time their songs?

SHORE LARK
L 16cm. Rare. Plain back, yellow and black on head. Saltmarsh on coast in winter.

MEADOW PIPIT
L 15cm. Slim, weak; song flight from and back to ground; shrill 'eep-eep-eep'.

TREE PIPIT
L 15cm. Sleek but stocky; song flight from and back to tree; 'tzeez' call.

CRESTED LARK
L 17cm. Not in UK. Pale sandy or orange-brown. Crest pointed. No white on wing or tail. Fluty call notes.

TAWNY PIPIT
L 17cm. Not in UK. Very pale with band of spots on wing. Long tail like wagtail.

ROCK PIPIT
L 16cm. Dark; smudgy streaks. Seashore. Call slurred 'feest'. Dark legs.

WOODLARK
L 15cm. Rare. Dumpy; short tail with pale corners. Black-and-white wing mark, rufous cheek. Beautiful song.

WATER PIPIT
L 16cm. Alps in summer; waterside in winter, when more streaked. Dark legs, white throat.

SWALLOW AND MARTINS

GENERAL HABITS

Not even the cuckoo is such a symbol of summer as the elegant, flowing lines of the swallow over a meadow, or dodging the players on a cricket field, as it swoops low over the grass catching insects. The house martin rarely flies so low, preferring rooftop height and sometimes almost out of sight high up with the swifts. Sand martins are usually near water and make tunnels for their nests in banks of earth or soft sandstone. In southern Europe there is also the crag martin, larger than a sand martin, with broader wings and an only slightly forked tail. It nests in mountains and on rocky coasts.

Swallows like lakes in spring, as there are more insects there, but in summer prefer fields with horses and cattle; they fly low and catch insects in the air. In the autumn large flocks gather on wires and roost in dense reedbeds.

FOOD AND FEEDING

These are all insect-eaters and feed on the wing. They never flit about among foliage (although they roost in reedbeds and perch on bare branches, which swifts *never* do).

SWALLOW
L 20cm. Long forked tail, dark throat, all-dark back (but white tail spots). Young bird has shorter tail.

HOUSE MARTIN ▷
L 12cm. Blue-black with brown wings, white rump; stiff-winged flutter and glide. Nests under eaves.

CRAG MARTIN ▲
L 13cm. Dark brown back, white spots on spread tail. Swooping, swingboat flight beside cliffs. Not UK.

◁ SAND MARTIN
L 12cm. Flicking flight quite weak; brown back and breast band. Waterside.

PROJECT

Learn to identify swifts, house and sand martins and swallows next spring. Swifts are easy; they fly high, or in flocks around rooftops, screaming as they go, and look black. Swallows look more supple, flowing low over the ground; house martins are stiffer and fluttery and have white on the lower back. Sand martins are smallest, flickery in flight, pale brown and white – they are the smallest swallow.

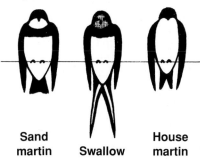

Sand martin   Swallow   House martin

Keep a diary of arrivals and departures. Sand martins are often the first migrants in spring, in early March; swallows (above) reach northwest Europe in early April, house martins a few days later; swifts are usually as late as May. Watch for them all over lakes and reservoirs where insects fly early in spring. Crag martins, not found in the UK, reach southern France and Italy early in spring; in Spain they stay all year.

WREN, ROBIN AND DUNNOCK

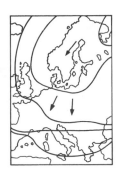

WAXWING
L 18cm. Usually very rare.
Dumpy, rounded or sleek.
Crest; short legs, short tail.
Black mask and chin.

GENERAL FEATURES

Robins are round or slim, depending on their
mood, but always lively, alert, even cheeky-
looking, with a frequent flick of the tail and
sharp 'tik' calls. Wrens are tiny, rounded, often
cock-tailed, with thin, pointed bills. The
dunnock is a hunched, slim-beaked, shuffling
little bird. Waxwings are like dumpy, colourful
starlings with short crests.

HABITS

Robins and wrens like shrubberies and woods,
but robins also come to lawns and birdtables.
Wrens forage in dense undergrowth, from
brambles and ivy to bracken on moors, but also
sing from tall trees. Dunnocks prefer the edges
of flowerbeds and hedges. Groups of waxwings,
surprisingly tame, feed on berries such as those
of cotoneaster and hawthorn.

When berries are abundant
in northern Europe,
waxwings stay there all
winter. In years when
waxwings have had a good
breeding season, and
numbers are high, but there
are few berries, they have to
move south in an 'eruption'.

Robins are particular favourites among bird-lovers. The robin is an unobtrusive bird, but not shy, with the male and female looking alike. What time of year do they sing? When do they stop? (Their song may sound different in the autumn.) In late summer they keep hidden while moulting, but you can look for brown-breasted young ones (right). How soon do they become red-breasted?

ROBIN ▶

L 14cm. Perky, round, flicks tail and wings; orange-red breast (spotted on young).

DUNNOCK ▼

L 14cm. Quiet, shuffling, dark grey and brown. Fine bill; reddish legs. Streaks.

WREN ▼

L 9cm. Tiny, round, cocked tail; scolding from bushes. Barred rusty-brown; thin bill.

HOW TO WATCH

Young robins are brown, spotty, with no red at first. Dunnocks (right) are darker, greyer and streaked. Sparrows are bigger, with thick bills, stronger streaking on top, and a broad pale band above the eye. Brown finches, such as young linnets, have triangular bills and forked tails, and often live in lively groups; robins and dunnocks never fly in flocks.

WAGTAILS AND DIPPER

YELLOW WAGTAIL
L 16cm. Elegant; quick and agile, on long, spindly legs. White edges to tail and marks on wing. Female is paler.

IDENTIFICATION

Wagtail identification is helped by the time of year. Yellow wagtails go to Africa in winter, so from October to March inclusive any wagtail with yellow on it should be a grey wagtail! Grey wagtails spend the summer along rushing rivers in hilly areas, or beside mill races, but move to lakes, ponds, and even puddles on flat roofs or in car parks in winter. Pied wagtails, which are black, grey and white, also like water and they, too, are often seen on tarmac, walking quickly about on footpaths, car parks and such places where few other birds feed.

HABITS

All wagtails have long, slim tails (longest in the grey wagtail) which they swing up and down as they walk. Yellow wagtails are especially fond of walking near farm animals, which disturb flies from the grass.

France

Scandinavia

Yellow wagtails come in different types depending on where they live. In the UK males have mostly yellow heads. In France they have blue-grey heads with a long stripe of white over each eye; in Spain blue with shorter white stripes; in Scandinavia darker grey without white. Greek ones are splendid, with glossy black heads.

PIED WAGTAIL ▶
L 18cm. UK males black on back; females greyer. European birds much paler grey.

pied (British)

♂ S

♀ W

white (Continental)

GREY WAGTAIL ▼
L 19cm. Yellow under tail; summer males yellow below with black chin, grey back.

♀

♂

DIPPER ▼
L 18cm. Always by water. Dumpy; big white chest patch. Young duller, spotty. Swims, even dives underwater. Bobs.

juv

HOW TO WATCH

A stream in the hills, where the water rushes between rocks, and alder trees overhang the banks, is perfect for summer birdwatching. Grey wagtails (right) and dippers are often together in such places, with pied wagtails usually not far away. If there are damp meadows beside the river, you may find yellow wagtails, too! In winter, reservoir edges, floodwater almost anywhere (from marshes to city streets) and modern sewage farms – with concrete tanks – all have wagtails from time to time.

CHATS

♀

REDSTART
L 14cm. Only summer male has black throat (speckled white in autumn). Female paler, browner. Likes old trees in woods or by heaths.

GENERAL FEATURES

These are all small relatives of the thrushes and look like them, but are usually shorter-tailed and more upright when they perch. Nightingales are plain but with redder tails; both redstarts have red on the tail and bluethroats have rusty tail patches.

HABITS

Whinchats and stonechats sit upright on tall, open stems and call loudly if disturbed. Nightingales sing beautifully in spring but keep well out of sight in dense bushes. Wheatears like stony places near areas of short grass in the hills, but turn up almost anywhere in spring and autumn. Bluethroats are scarce and hard to see, often in thick cover at the edges of reedbeds. Black redstarts prefer Continental villages, factories or quarries, but redstarts are

Redstart habits
Redstarts are gorgeous birds of old woods, but turn up on the coast in autumn when migrating. They always shiver their tails in a quivering up-and-down movement. Often perching inside the foliage of a tree, they fly out into open spaces to catch flies, or even flit down to the ground for a moment to pick up food. They may give away their presence by a short, loud whistle followed by several ticking notes.

WHINCHAT
L 12cm. Not winter; pale stripe over eye, mask on male. White patches on tail. Sits on top of tall stems and bracken.

BLACK REDSTART
L 14cm. Males black with white in wing, female and young smoky-grey; rusty tail.

STONECHAT
L 12cm. All year; dark head including chin; female browner. Sits on top of gorse or tall stems on heaths.

WHEATEAR
L 15cm. Black T on striking white rear. Male clean grey, black and cream.

BLUETHROAT
L 15cm. Rare in UK. Red patches each side of tail, breast marked with black (blue on spring male). Very secretive.

NIGHTINGALE
L 16cm. Like large robin with greyer head, rufous tail. Brilliant song from thicket.

THRUSHES

FIELDFARE
L 25cm. Big thrush with grey head and rump; black on face; bright breast spotted black, belly pure white.

GENERAL HABITS

Thrushes are widespread throughout the world, and there are some little-known species in Asia. In Europe, though, they tend to be familiar garden or woodland birds, some moving south and west each winter into areas where they don't breed. There is one exception, the ring ouzel, which migrates south in winter and moves north in spring to remote upland crags. The blackbird is one of Europe's commonest birds, at home in gardens and one of the best songsters. Song thrushes are usually scarcer, but still common and widespread and also brilliant singers. The mistle thrush is bigger, far less numerous, and with a very loud voice.

Fieldfares nest in groups, and in autumn form flocks to migrate westwards to milder regions. In winter the large, chattering flocks are on ploughed fields or grassland, flying to tall hedges and trees nearby when disturbed.

WINTER ROAMERS

Fieldfares and redwings breed on the Continent and arrive in flocks in the UK in October, to roam fields and hedges for berries and worms.

BLACKBIRD
L 26cm. Male all black except for yellow bill, eye-rings; female brown, chin pale, spotted; young rusty.

You will often hear a song thrush feeding! Loud, sharp smacks reveal a song thrush whacking a big garden snail against a stone or paving slab, to break into its shell. Why not make daily counts of snails at the 'anvil' and try to identify which ones the song thrush is eating? Does the number of snails change with the seasons?

RING OUZEL
L 24cm. Male black, white breast crescent, paler wings; female has pale scaly marks, pale edges on wing feathers.

REDWING
L 21cm. Small, dark; broad white stripe over eye, rufous underwing. Winter in UK.

SONG THRUSH
L 23cm. Small; warm brown. V-shaped spots, plain tail; common garden thrush.

MISTLE THRUSH
L 27cm. Large, greyish; big rounded spots; whitish edges to tail, streaky wings.

juv

WARBLERS

WELL-KNOWN SONGS

Waterside and marshland warblers are often hard to tell apart. However, only reed and sedge warblers are very common. Sedge warblers have very varied, joyful songs, while reeds have a more repetitive, rhythmic song with a harsh, less 'happy' effect, often given by a bird just out of sight below the tops of tall reeds. Sedge warblers sing from hawthorn bushes and all kinds of waterside vegetation, as well as in a special song flight.

RARER VOICES

Grasshopper warblers make a remarkable noise, a fast, metallic trill that goes on without change or pause for minutes on end, a little like a freewheeling bicycle. Cetti's warblers are rare in Britain but commoner in southern Europe; they have a short but very loud song – it is a real outburst of fast, liquid notes.

Reed and sedge warblers sing loudly from dense waterside vegetation, but only the sedge warbler flies up to sing in a short, jerky display flight, head up and wings fluttering.

SEDGE WARBLER
L 12cm. Lively, restless, in nettles, reeds; white stripe over eye, pale rusty-buff rump; slightly streaked.

REED WARBLER ▷
L 12cm. Plain brown on top, only slight stripe over eye; reeds and nearby willows.

GRASSHOPPER WARBLER
L 12cm. Tapered tail; softly streaked back, wings. High, prolonged reeling song.

MARSH WARBLER
L 12cm. Very rare in UK. Like reed, but song more varied.

CETTI'S WARBLER ▲
L 14cm. Rare in UK. Red-brown and whitish; dark round tail. Very loud, abrupt song.

SAVI'S WARBLER ▷
L 14cm. Like large red-brown reed, with rounder tail; insect-like buzzing song.

PROJECT

Except for Cetti's, these warblers arrive in late April and sing until summer. They sing best early in the morning but also in the daytime. Find a small reedbed beside a slow river or lake, and let the birds (like this sedge warbler) come to the reed tops.

WARBLERS

L 14cm. Longish tail; alert, lively; sings with puffed-out throat, swings tail. Dives into brambles. Male has grey head. All have white chin, rufous on wings.

♂   ♀

GENERAL FEATURES

The warblers are divided into several groups. The slim, greenish ones which slip easily through the foliage of trees and bushes (such as the willow warbler) are 'leaf warblers' and make soft 'hooeet' calls. The whitethroats, blackcap and garden warbler are in a different group, and they make hard, sharp calls like a piece of wood tapped on a stone – 'tak'. These calls help track them down in the dense undergrowth they often inhabit.

AUTUMN BEHAVIOUR

In the autumn practically all the warblers can be seen in lower bushes and weedy places, eagerly eating soft berries such as honeysuckle and elder. Watching an elder bush with plenty of fruit is often the best way to study them.

Bushy places with rough grass clearings, brambles scrambling between hawthorn and blackthorn thickets, nettle beds and patches of gorse are the places to look for whitethroats. Lesser whitethroats prefer less open areas, old gardens, woodland edges and thick shrubberies, and shady lanes with tall, dense hedges. Whitethroats often perch on wires and sing in flight; lessers keep much more hidden away.

WILLOW WARBLER
L 11cm. Olive; young yellower. Pale legs; lovely descending song.

CHIFFCHAFF
L 11cm. Dull olive; dark legs; repetitive 'chip chap chap chip' song.

GARDEN WARBLER
L 14cm. Dull, pale, neat; thickish bill, beady eye. Superb song in trees, bushes.

BLACKCAP
L 14cm. Grey male has black cap, browner female brown cap; brilliant song from trees in leafy woods.

WOOD WARBLER
L 12cm. Bright green, yellow and white; streaked wings. Song a tinny trill.

♀

♂

LESSER WHITETHROAT
L 13cm. Neat, clean look; grey-brown wings; dark legs; white throat.

DARTFORD WARBLER
L 13cm. Dark grey-brown above, reddish below; long tail. Short, hard song.

FLYCATCHERS AND OTHERS

PIED FLYCATCHER

Pied flycatchers are migrants, so can appear in out-of-the-way places in spring and, especially, in the autumn, when they tend to turn up in bushy or wooded areas by the coast. In summer they like old oak woods in the north and west, and can be attracted to nest in them by special nestbox schemes. Males are black and white in spring and summer, but become brown and white in autumn (still with white forehead spots, which separate them from the females). Despite their bold pattern, they are not easy to see in the contrasting sun and shade of a dense wood.

Spotted flycatchers like to nest in a shallow box or old nest, or make a nest of their own in a creeper, so they can see over the rim; even an old discarded bean tin may be used at times!

SPOTTED FLYCATCHER

Spotted flycatchers are much more widespread than pieds, often nesting in parks and large gardens. They are very late migrants, often arriving at the end of May.

juv

♀

♂

PIED FLYCATCHER
L 12cm. White below, white wing patch; catches flies in mid air or on ground. Female brown where male is black. Young spotted above, white areas more buff.

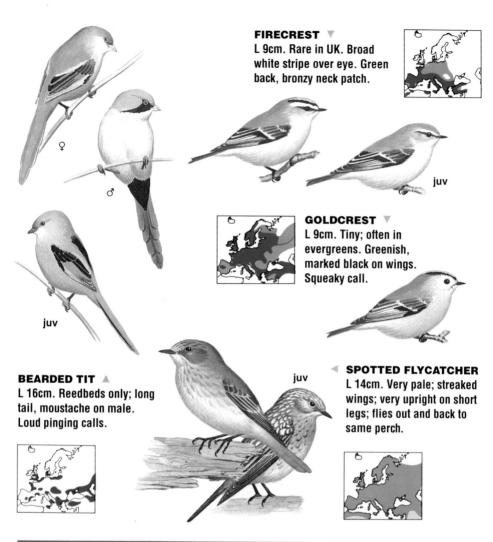

FIRECREST

L 9cm. Rare in UK. Broad white stripe over eye. Green back, bronzy neck patch.

juv

GOLDCREST

L 9cm. Tiny; often in evergreens. Greenish, marked black on wings. Squeaky call.

♀

♂

juv

BEARDED TIT

L 16cm. Reedbeds only; long tail, moustache on male. Loud pinging calls.

juv

SPOTTED FLYCATCHER

L 14cm. Very pale; streaked wings; very upright on short legs; flies out and back to same perch.

HOW TO WATCH

Goldcrests (right) and firecrests are hard to see, as they keep to the tops of tall trees, particularly conifers. At certain times, especially in autumn, they come to low bushes and are often very tame. Listen for their high, thin, 'zee-zee-zee' calls and look for them with flocks of tits. They are the smallest European birds.

TITS

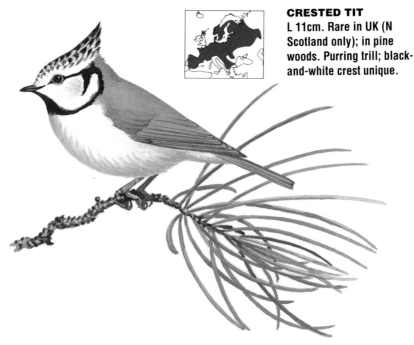

HABITS

The tit family includes some of our most familiar and popular birds, which nest in boxes that we make for them and feed at special feeders that we put out for them. Make a birdtable and put out bags of peanuts (from dealers approved by the Birdfood Standards Association) between about October and March; but don't feed them in spring – the nuts can easily choke baby birds.

AUTUMN BEHAVIOUR

In autumn tits join together in mixed flocks (sometimes with treecreepers, flycatchers, even woodpeckers tagging along, too) and roam around the woods looking for food. A wood can seem empty until you suddenly find yourself surrounded by small birds – then, in a few minutes, they are all gone.

Crested tits make their nest by digging a hole in a rotten tree stump, usually a pine. Sometimes they use other trees, or even wooden posts.

BLUE TIT
L 11cm. Tiny; brightest in spring, blue and yellow. Blue cap, white face.

WILLOW TIT
L 11cm. Small but bull-necked; dull cap, pale wing panel, brighter sides. Loud, nasal buzzing calls.

MARSH TIT
L 11cm. Small, pale; shiny black cap. Loud 'pit-chu' call. In ones and twos.

GREAT TIT
L 14cm. Strong; black head with white cheeks, black stripe down body. Noisy.

LONG-TAILED TIT
L 14cm (mostly tail). Ball-and-stick shape. Unique. Thin, high calls and stutter.

PROJECT

Make a nestbox for blue tits. Use good-quality wood or exterior plywood. The box should be at least 12cm square inside, and the hole must be 20cm above the floor. Make the hole 3cm wide. Put the box out of reach of passers-by and cats, if you can.

COAL TIT
L 11cm. Tiny; buff underneath; no yellow, green or blue. Wingbars; white square on back of neck.

SHRIKES, ORIOLE AND OTHERS

GOLDEN ORIOLE
L 24cm. Male brilliant;
female greener, rump yellow
like green woodpecker's (so
beware wishful thinking!).

GENERAL FEATURES

This is a mixed bunch, the nuthatch being like
a small, agile woodpecker (but able to hop in
all directions as it doesn't use its tail as a prop);
the treecreepers have curved bills and sit back
on their tails. Golden orioles are thrush-like,
with stouter bills and longer wings. Shrikes
have long tails, short wings, and stout,
slightly hooked bills.

HABITS

Nuthatches like large trees and hop about the
branches, and also come to peanut bags. The
treecreepers shuffle about close to the bark,
probing for insects; they don't come to feeders.
Orioles keep to the tops of leafy trees such as
poplars. Shrikes sit on exposed perches and dart
after large insects on the ground or small birds.

Treecreepers are always
clinging to bark (or, rarely,
an old wall), searching up,
around, then down to the
next tree, for tiny insects and
spiders. Big ornamental
Wellingtonia trees with soft
bark are used for roosting;
treecreepers hollow out egg-
shaped holes and cling
inside them overnight.

NUTHATCH ▶
L 14cm. In old woods; slaty-grey and buff. Jerky hops up, down, along branches.

WOODCHAT SHRIKE ▲
L 18cm. Rare in UK. Black and white with red-brown cap. Perches upright.

GREAT GREY SHRIKE ▲
L 24cm. Winter only in UK. Pale grey, black, white, with long, swinging tail, black mask. Often on bush tops.

◀ ## RED-BACKED SHRIKE
L 17cm. Rare UK. Red-brown; male with black mask on pale head, female barred.

TREECREEPER
L 12cm. Woods; shuffles upwards on bark, using tail as prop. Spirals around branches.

SHORT-TOED TREECREEPER ▶
L 12cm. Not in UK. Like dull treecreeper, whitest on throat. Very difficult.

CROWS

JAY
L 35cm. Lovely pink, black and white, with blue on wing. White rump most obvious. Often on ground, but shy; quickly flies into trees.

GENERAL FEATURES

Crows are few people's favourites, but they are characters, intelligent and lively. Jays are extremely beautiful, too, and even the magpie is a magnificent bird, fortunately again becoming common after much persecution.

IN REMOTE PLACES

The chough is a rare crow with splendidly glossy plumage and wild, extrovert behaviour as it zooms about on the wind currents around the cliffs it inhabits. To see the raven, you have to visit remote coastal cliffs, or high crags in the hills. This is a big bird, with far-carrying calls and great powers of flight. It even turns upside down as it flies, as if for sheer fun.

Jays (and sometimes starlings) have a very curious habit, which you may be lucky enough to see in a park or on a large lawn where there are ants. The bird will stand on the ground, stretching up, but with its wings half open and its head bent down. Then it will pick up ants in its bill and put them on to its feathers. It lets ants crawl all over it. Maybe the formic acid from the ants keeps the feathers in good condition, or kills tiny ticks and mites that live in them.

MAGPIE
L 45cm. Very long tail; large white patches. Rattled 'chaka chaka chaka' call.

RAVEN
L 65cm. Very big; likes remote places. Diamond-shaped tail, long wings, large head.

ROOK
L 45cm. Flocks; baggy trousers, pointed bill with white face. Rounded tail. Nests in treetop colonies.

CARRION CROW
L 47cm. All black, or half-black and half-grey; no white on face. Square tail.

CHOUGH
L 37cm. Rare, on cliffs. Curved red bill and vivid red legs. Acrobatic flight.

juv

JACKDAW
L 33cm. Cheerful, bouncy dark-grey crow, paler hood. Quick flight, pigeon-like.

juv

SPARROWS AND FINCHES

LIVELY SPARROWS

Sparrows are cheeky, active, quarrelsome birds.
Tree sparrows are much scarcer than house
sparrows, best identified by their brown caps
and black cheek spots, and always good to find
in mixed finch and sparrow flocks on farmland.
Sparrows, more than any other birds, cheep
and chirp – there is no other way to describe it!
Even their songs, such as they are, are simple,
repetitive chirrups. But the tree sparrow has
another, distinctive call – a hard 'tek tek'.
House sparrows form flocks in cornfields in late
summer, flying up in dense clouds when
alarmed.

Sparrows delight in a bird
bath and splash water
through their feathers in a
thorough 'wash'. This keeps
their plumage in good
condition. They also 'bathe'
in dust: on dry days, look for
them in hollows in dusty
flowerbeds.

SPECIAL FINCHES

Crossbills are chunky, large-headed finches of
conifer forests. They use the crossed tips of their
unusual bills to prise open scales on pine cones,
then scoop out the seeds with their tongues.

HOUSE SPARROW
L 15cm. Bright, cheerful,
cocky; male has black bib,
grey band along top of head.
Female pale brown, dull buff
below; streaked back; broad
pale stripe over eye.

HAWFINCH
L 16cm. Shy. Thick-set; broad white wing band. White tail-tip. Ticking calls.

W

S

STARLING ▲
L 21cm. Noisy, quarrelsome; short tail. Spotted in winter.

TREE SPARROW ▲
L 14cm. Neat; brown cap, black cheek spot. Female the same. Farms and parkland.

♂ **W**

♂ **S**

BRAMBLING ◀
L 14cm. White rump, orange wing patch. Male black on head in spring.

♀

BULLFINCH ◀
L 14cm. Stout; big white rump. Male pinky-red, female duller; black cap and chin.

♂

♀

CROSSBILL ▶
L 16cm. Specialised pine- and spruce-cone feeder; feeds quietly but drops cones. Flies with loud 'chip chip' calls.

♂

♀

CHAFFINCH ▲
L 14cm. Green rump, white wing patch; male pink on breast. Female olive, white wingbars.

♂

♀

FINCHES

GOLDFINCH
L 12cm. Adult unique, red, black and white face; broad band of yellow on wing. Young plainer brown, but still yellow in wings.

juv

GENERAL FEATURES

Finches are small, gregarious birds, most of them with attractive, brightly coloured plumage. If you learn their different ways of behaving, you can tell finches apart even without seeing their colours.

BEHAVIOUR

Some, like the chaffinch, feed in groups but fly up a few at a time and move separately. Others, such as greenfinches and linnets, form tighter flocks which fly up in a single group. Goldfinches have a lively flight, little groups bounding between patches of thistles. Siskins zoom out of one treetop in a tightly-packed flock, away into the distance, only to swing back and pour into the top of another tree.

Hawfinches (above) take big, tough seeds and fruit stones. The greenfinch is also strong, but the bullfinch (top) rolls soft buds in its gentler bill to clean off the scales. Goldfinches reach into thistle heads to tease out seeds in their pointed bills.

GREENFINCH
L 14cm. Yellow wing and tail patches; unstreaked. Male greenest, young browner.

PROJECT

Look for greenfinch colonies (usually only two or three pairs nesting fairly close together) around tall, leafy old limes and sycamores, big hawthorn hedges, churchyard yew trees and such places. Watch males (below) displaying, especially their song flights.

♂ S

REDPOLL ▶
L 12cm. Tiny; streaked, with black chin, dark red cap. Pink breast in spring.

♂ S

♂   ♀

TWITE ▶
L 13cm. Streaky brown; plain orange throat. White in wings and tail.

SERIN ▲
L 11cm. Not UK. Tiny, streaky; yellow rump. Male has yellow face and chest.

LINNET ▼
L 13cm. Male grey on head, red chest in spring; female streaky. White both in wings and tail.

♀   ♂

♀   ♂

SISKIN ▲
L 12cm. Tiny; green. Male has lime-green chest. Yellow on wings and tail.

BUNTINGS

GENERAL FEATURES

Buntings are rather finch-like but subtly different. Most have slightly longer tails, with prominent white sides (such as the reed bunting). They tend to have narrower, slightly more pointed heads and slimmer bills, and make more metallic, ticking calls, but it is not easy to say why a finch is not a bunting or vice versa.

HABITS

You will often find finches and buntings together, but, if a mixed flock flies up, the buntings often go off on their own and keep separate from the more panicky finches. Buntings somehow seem to have a lazier lifestyle – none more so than the yellowhammer that sits on a bush top all summer long and sings over and over again, long after most birds have stopped!

Snow buntings
Snow buntings are special birds of the coast, and must be looked for late in the autumn and in winter. In some years they are very scarce, in others quite frequent, with large flocks bounding along the shingle ridges or over saltmarsh pools like flurries of snow. They make two very characteristic calls that help to locate them: a fluty, liquid 'tyoow' and a rippling, tinkling trill.

SNOW BUNTING
L 17cm. Coasts in winter. Mixed red-brown, sandy-brown, black and white; oldest males whitest. Most white shows in flight.

W ♂

W ♀

REED BUNTING
L 15cm. Wet places; black and white head on spring male. Black tail edged white.

CORN BUNTING
L 18cm. Big; pale, streaky brown, no white in tail. Big pale bill.

CIRL BUNTING
L 16cm. Rare UK. Black and yellow head on male; female streaked, olive rump.

YELLOWHAMMER
L 16cm. Male yellow, streaked black above; female streaked, red-brown rump. White sides to long tail.

LAPLAND BUNTING
L 15cm. Rare. Streaked, with black on face, reddish band across wing. Coasts.

W ♂

ORTOLAN BUNTING
L 16cm. Rare UK. Pale eye-ring; pink bill. Male greenish and orange on head.

S ♂

INDEX

ILLUSTRATIONS BY

Bernard Thornton Artists: Jim Channell 14–15, 82–83; Robert Morton 8–9, 22–23 · Garden Studios: Shirley Felts cover; Steve Holden 24–31, 36–39 · Karen Johnson 69 (top) · Ian Lewington 40, 56, 66–68, 78, 86, 90–91, 98, 108–124 · Linden Artists: Stephen Lings 44–48, 58–62, 70, 74, 76, 80, 84, 92, 100, 102–104; Jane Pickering 6–7, 10–12, 16–17; Phil Weare 20–21, 32–35; David Webb 4–5 · Maltings Partnership 18–19, 87. Additional black and white line illustrations by Karen Johnson. All other illustrations by Ian Willis.

The publishers would like to thank the following organisations and individuals for their kind permission to reproduce the photographs in this book:

Eric and David Hosking 55, 67, 73 · Frank Lane Picture Agency: Front Cover; W.S. Clark 49; S. Jonasson 43; Silvestris 93; Roger Tidman 76; Terry Whittaker 27; Roger Wilmhurst 75 · Nature Photographers: 95; F.V. Blackburn 13 centre, 110, 113; Kevin Carlson 44; Colin Carver 114; Hugh Clark 91; Andrew Cleave 35; R.H. Fisher 79; C.H. Gomersall 101 below; E.A. Janes 21, 49; Chris and Jo Knights 69; R. Mearns 13 top; O. Newman 52, 109; Philip J. Newman 81; W.S. Paton 17; J.F. Reynolds 70; Robert T. Smith 65; Paul Sterry 89, 103; Roger Tidman 33, 37, 58, 71, 78, 101 above, 106; Maurice Walker 123; Derek Washington 115; Jonathan Wilson 45 · NHPA: Henry Ausloos 47; G.I. Bernard 7; John Buckingham 83; Laurie Campbell 23, 107; Stephen Dalton 99; Melvin Grey 51; Brian Hawkes 57; E.A. Janes 9, 13 below; Michael Leach 61, 63; Jonathan Wilson 31.